ESCAPE
TO THAILAND
by
Matt Owens Rees
© Matt Owens Rees 2013

If you enjoyed this book, please encourage your friends to purchase and download their own copy and take a look at its companion volumes: *Thailand Take Two, A Thailand Diary, The Thai Way of Meekness*, and the novel *The Death of a Thai Godfather*

Thank you for your support.

Table of Contents

Introduction

Conclusion

About the Author

Extracts from other Books by Matt Owens Rees

Introduction

Names have been changed but *Escape to Thailand* is a true biographical account of an English expat's experiences, frustrations, and hopes on moving permanently to Thailand. It is written by Matt Owens Rees from interviews and from references to Derek's diaries, and is from his perspective. Some expats may relate similar experiences; others may have widely different observations on their life here. Try to put yourself in Derek's shoes and ask yourself if you would have done anything differently.

Following a bitter divorce and a forced early retirement from his job in a bank, Derek struggles with making the final decision to leave England for good and settle for the rest of his life in Thailand. We begin to understand the turmoil going on in his head when he realises what he is leaving behind in the land of his birth. We see from his questioning that he is still unsure whether he is doing the right thing or not.

He explains how he felt about some of the cultural differences that awaited him and how he coped with them. He compares them with the very different experiences that some of his expat friends encountered. Culture shock is not the same for everyone. We see him getting to grips with his new life but is he really settled here? Are there going to be some unpleasant surprises in store for him? Who is wearing the trousers? He or the Thai lady he was meeting.

Was he seeing only the acceptable parts of Thai life? *Escape to Thailand* is not judgmental. It leaves the reader to consider and try to understand the way events were unfolding. The problems of Thai and western relationships, even if they seem to be surmountable in the short term, are brought out in Derek's true account of his early days in Thailand.

With many glimpses into the lives of ordinary Thais, the biography becomes a "fly on the wall" experience for the reader. Seeing what the average tourist or visitor rarely sees.

Chapter 1 We Are Airborne

An inner voice was telling me. "Get off this plane now." But it was too late. Thai Airways Flight TG 911 was preparing for take-off. Rather an unfortunate flight number given the events in America in 2001. The 747 jumbo let loose the power of its four engines with a roar. With the brakes released, all 340 or so passengers, including me, were forced back into their seats as we gathered speed down runway 2 at London's Heathrow Airport and started the ascent into the mid-morning sky.

I was embarking on a 6000 mile trip for a blind date with a young woman, much younger than I was, that I had met on an internet-dating site. She had invited me over to Thailand on two previous occasions. I declined them all. This time, for reasons I was still uncertain of, I had decided to take up her offer. But was I thinking straight?

Three years later, I had learned that it was Toy's daughter, Kanya, who had encouraged her mother to "find a new husband for yourself and a father for me. Let's be a family together again." Sitting in my seat now, I was, of course, unaware of that.

Toy had seemed intrigued in chatting to a foreigner over the internet. Thais have this perception that all *farangs* (white foreigners) are rich, not appreciating that high wages also come with high taxes and a high cost of living. English men particularly are seen as more honest and caring than Thai men – the Thai expression is *poo dee angkrit*. It has no direct translation but implies a feeling that Westerners are trustworthy and malleable. That they can be easily manipulated and persuaded to be fairly compliant with a wife's demands. Very unlike the way a woman is able to treat a Thai man.

Toy was six thousand miles away, but for me it was as if she was sitting right next to me. I thought that a certain chemistry was beginning to develop for both of us. And we had never actually met! We started to understand our different national cultures, though I was to learn a lot more sometime later about how different Thais are from Westerners.

But now, Thai Airways flight TG 911 bound for Bangkok was airborne and I was securely strapped into my seat. I started thinking whether I was taking a big chance on this blind date. Would others have booked and paid for a long haul flight to meet someone they had never met face to face and had never spoken to? Had I completely thought this position through? Was the nastiness of my divorce clouding my rational thinking?

I gulped down yet another complimentary double scotch and hoped it would help me relax on what I was beginning to think would be a boring and tedious flight into the unknown. I was embarking on a 12000 mile round trip for a blind date with a young woman, much younger than me, that I had met only on an internet-dating site. She had invited me over to Thailand on two previous occasions. I declined them all. This time, for reasons I was still uncertain of, I had decided to take up her offer. But was I thinking straight?

After 16 years, like so many other marriages it would seem, mine had suddenly hit a brick wall. With a divorce finalised and a major slice of my working life completed, I was facing a financial and personal crisis that I could not see my way around. The only matter that remained following the divorce was the sale of the matrimonial home, and this was becoming a very protracted and tiresome concern. I was lucky to some extent, the house was large enough for both of us to lead separate lives. I lived in the self-contained granny annex. It became my sanctuary after the decree absolute. She lived in the main house. I was able to lead a near-normal life, returning home late into the evening after a long day at the office. Like many fathers, I saw my young son only at weekends.

My ex-wife, however, seemed to be making sure that my son was fully committed in doing something else whenever I was around.

She was leaving me very little time with him. I could see that this was going to be the pattern for the future. The only opportunities she allowed me to have with my son were when she decided she wanted to socialise and go out on the town. In her eyes, I was just the convenient unpaid baby sitter.

If I was ever delayed through being caught up in a traffic jam, she was always quick to point the nagging finger and say that I did not care a jot for my son. If it spoilt her planned excursions into the night, it was always down to me. My neighbours, whom I had known for years, could often see me driving at break neck speed to return home, screeching down our drive just as she was bundling him in the car to dump him at a friend's home for the evening. Nothing was going to spoil her own pre-planned evening soirée. Michael would be left, without company of his own age, with an old family he hardly knew.

She could do as she wanted. I could not be even two or three minutes late. My neighbours were sympathetic and could see what was going on. However, there was nothing anyone could do to counter the devious game she was determined to play.

My ex-wife was 10 years younger than I was. Although she was always a little spoilt, we had had some good times together, and she did not lack for anything a young bride could wish for. I had a good job and every penny of my salary was spent on our home. She had every modern expensive appliance she wanted, mirroring the life style she was leaving behind at her parents' home.

She wanted everything that I had provided for our lives together to remain solely with her. And that included Michael. She did not want me to be part of our son's life. That was the rub. I was seeing a side of her that I had never seen before. I still don't understand why she was so scheming and had so much venom in her blood. Were her friends egging her on to cause trouble?

The days passed by as we waited for a buyer to be found for the home. She appeared to be disinclined to sell and always put on a sour face when potential buyers were viewing the property. The days turned to months, and the months into years. Living in this way and trying to hold down a job at the same time was not easy. My health began to suffer. I collapsed in the office twice in as many weeks. I got up and carried on with the job. I was never one to give in. My colleagues told me I needed to see a doctor. I made an appointment for the next day.

I had never seen my doctor so concerned. After taking my blood pressure and checking my pulse, he asked me questions about my life style and what problems I had. Without saying a word, he wrote out a prescription to help with my obvious stress, and insisted I stop work for at least a month.

My lodgings now became my prison. I diligently took the medication prescribed but found myself sitting alone staring out of the window into the garden for hours at a time. My mind was in turmoil and I needed to do something as this was the first time in my thirty-four year working life that I had ever been signed off by a doctor. I was used to working a normal 7 hour day. Now my life was at a standstill. I had pleaded with my doctor not to keep me from work, as this was my only outlet for normality.

During my forced imprisonment, I sought refuge in my computer. It was to become my lifeline. Music from my CD collection was my sole companion. Sport and news on my small television set; my only contact with the outside world. Surfing the net one day, I stumbled on a travel site about countries in the Far East. It was most interesting. There was a clip of people enjoying what seemed to be a very stress free and happy existence. No worries, no stress, everyone appeared to be living a life without a care in the world. How I wished my life could be like that. Why can't everyone live in that sort of harmony? Totally different from my situation: sitting in front of a computer, not knowing what the future was holding for me, nothing to look
forward to. I surfed a bit more in my boredom. Then, somehow, I got onto a Thai social networking site and started chatting with some people.

I started feeling less lonely, that someone out there was caring enough to talk to me. A lady called *Tasanee* was on line. Obviously

Thai, but I had no idea how you would pronounce her name. I laughed aloud when she wrote that she also had a nickname and was called Toy by her friends. We have nicknames in the West, of course. I had one in school but I'm not telling you what it was. Apparently, in Thailand everyone has a nickname and they use it in place of their given first name, which is really only used for official documents.

That was my first contact with Toy and the first time I had laughed aloud for a very long time.
Even now, I find it difficult to express the impact that my first excursion into Thailand, albeit a virtual excursion over a computer connection, had on me. It was a very positive experience. My life was returning. Or was I clutching at straws?

Toy was a 39-year-old teacher from the Northern Thai province of Chiangmai. She had one daughter; I had one son. I did not know the detail at the time but I sensed she had gone through a rough patch in her marriage prior to her husband's premature death in a road accident. Being 10 years widowed, she had thrown herself into her teaching and bringing up her daughter, Kanya. From our exchange of messages over the internet, she came across as someone who genuinely wanted to settle down and enjoy once again living in a warm family environment. And at the time I didn't think I was wrong in my judgment.

Family is very important to a Thai. The strong bonds within the family are not easily understood by Westerners who are more self-dependent and don't feel family ties so strongly.
Messaging on the internet, Toy began telling me about her married life with her late husband, Somchai. Her marriage to a Thai man had not been without its problems. She was going to be cautious about any future friendship and not make another mistake in her life. Realising that a life without Kanya as her companion was fast approaching, she saw the logic of what her daughter was saying. Kanya was becoming more independent and sooner or later would be making her own way in life. Toy had to start looking at her future.

She seemed intrigued in chatting to a foreigner over the internet. Thais have this perception that all *farangs* (white foreigners) are rich, not appreciating that high wages also come with high taxes and a high cost of living. English men particularly are seen as more honest and caring than Thai men – the Thai expression is *poo dee angkrit*. It has no direct translation but implies a feeling that English men are trustworthy and malleable. That they can be easily manipulated and persuaded to be fairly compliant with a wife's demands. Very unlike the way a woman is able to treat a Thai man.

It was with Kanya's help that Toy had found this social networking site. Actually, it was more like a dating agency. Toy and I chatted a lot over the next six months, getting to know each other better. Behind the scenes, I later found out, Kanya was vetting some of the contacts on her mother's behalf. Sometimes, when Toy was busy, Kanya was replying to e-mails and instant messages herself. Including mine! Perhaps I should have seen that as a possible red light and thought more deeply about it; but I did not.

"Why not come over to Thailand and we can meet each other?" I suppose that the question was bound to crop up at some point but I was still a bit wary. It was a long way to travel. Although I had travelled before quite extensively, this was going to be my first long haul trip. I admit to some fear and trepidation. I thought of many reasons why I could not go at this time. The house had still not been sold. I had to consider how best to maintain my relationship with my son in the difficult circumstances that my ex-wife was creating. I wanted to meet Toy and Kanya, but how would I feel when the day came that I would have to return and resume my granny annex existence. My mind was not clear what I should do. Would there be difficulties in
being in a relationship with someone of a different culture? I declined the offer. The Christmases after my divorce were like ordinary days of the week for me. Sitting on my own, allowing the contents of a bottle to block out the unhappiness I felt about the way my life was going. The two days in every year; which for most of us are fuelled with food, wine, and much laughter between family and friends, were for me days I would rather forget. I had cooked myself

chicken and chips for my Christmas lunch. I enjoyed the meal but I was uneasy and not content with my life.

The TV's usual seasonal merriment failed to make any impression on me. Soon the programmes were a blur and I drifted into an alcohol-induced sleep. My ex-wife promised me that I could see my son over the Christmas and New Year period but she changed her mind at the last minute. Now I could see him only on New Year's Eve. She had a party to attend and did not want to miss it. I would be the babysitter.

I had been divorced for three years when Toy suggested for the third time that I visit her in Thailand. Having experienced the saddest days of my life, I accepted. I had to do something positive. Where was my life leading? I booked a ticket for 10 March. Her fortieth birthday was on the fourteenth and I was determined to celebrate the event with her and, in some small measure, repay the consideration she had been showing me during our chatting and messaging. I had no idea how birthdays are celebrated in Thailand but I was resolved to make it a happy occasion for her.

But now, Thai Airways flight TG 911 bound for Bangkok was airborne and I was securely strapped into my seat. I started thinking whether I was taking a big chance on this blind date. Would others have booked and paid for a long haul flight to meet someone they had never met face to face and had never spoken to? Had I completely thought this position through? Was the nastiness of my divorce clouding my rational thinking?

And that was when the voice inside me kept saying, *Get off this plane now.*

Chapter 2   A Blind Date

I did not know precisely what was awaiting me in Thailand. I had seen Toy's photograph. It was in my wallet. I felt I had got to know her well through our contact over the computer network. Remember, though, I had never heard her voice or seen her face to face. Would the chemistry still work when we actually met? What would she think of me? What if this did not work out? I could feel my heart pounding and it was pointless trying to sleep. I was even feeling a little scared about this whole adventure.

The sky was an unblemished blue and the brilliant sunlight was such a contrast to the dark and dismal tunnel that I had been living in for the last three years. I realised that this could be the escape that I was looking for. A chance to get my life back. I hoped it was what Toy wanted too. I no longer wanted the plane to turn around and drop me back on English soil. I was determined to put the past behind me and be positive for the future. My torments and unhappiness could stay behind at Heathrow airport. I was well rid of them. Only a few members of my family knew I was leaving for a twelve-day holiday. "Enjoy. Forget your problems for a while. Come back fully refreshed. The break will do you good." I was beginning to feel more relaxed and drifted into a light sleep. And I knew that if I did dream at all, they would be pleasant dreams and not horrific nightmares.

"Wake up, sir. We're serving breakfast." The smiling flight attendant helped me pull down the tray on the back of the seat in front of me and carefully placed my plate of bacon and eggs on it. She was wearing a long silk dress in the traditional Thai style. All the cabin crew looked smart in their uniforms and the female staff were drop dead gorgeous. Looking out of the window, I saw Thailand for the first time. The sun was slowly rising and I could see cars, looking like small toys, heading along the roads beneath me. The Chao Phraya River was alive with ships and boats starting to ply their early morning trade. What a colourful sight it made, merging with the many golden temples and other buildings sparkling in the first rays of the early morning sun.

We started to skim over shacks, housing complexes, rivers, markets, and factories. Amazing Thailand. Slums and temples. Lots of commotion and activity side by side with the picturesque gardens of Thailand's élite and the eye-catching images of the temples and monuments.

Thailand, like all Asian countries, held a great deal of fascination and interest for me. I was always glued to a book, the TV, or more recently the internet, when anything was said or printed about countries in the Far East. I had indeed spent many hours on the internet since accepting Toy's invitation, reading everything I could about the country and its culture. I realise now that I was getting addicted. Was I in danger of only seeing the rosy side of Thailand?

I had read many stories of money grabbing Asian women ready to scam so-called rich western men, offering endless love and then moving quickly on to the next victim once the money had dried up. Thai women, so it was portrayed in print, would shift from one western male to another, seeing each as a mobile ATM until such times as the card is refused. The boyfriend or husband swiftly became the ex-boyfriend or ex-husband. Out of love and out of cash. The Thai internet forums, and books such as Private Dancer, were full of tales of men being misled and cheated. Some stories on the forums were exaggerated but I began to think that some were true.

Looking around me, I could see several foreign men sitting alone. My thoughts turned to what I had been reading on the web. Perhaps some of these men would fall into the clutches of such scheming women and be left broken hearted and penniless. Was I going to meet that very fate myself? Were Toy and Kanya looking for the proverbial "sugar daddy?" I was convinced that they were not.

The plane had now touched down and, as the cabin door was opened, a gush of hot air wafted into the cabin. I had not appreciated how hot this country was, even in early morning. That initial surprise was my first introduction to Thailand. The memory will stay with me always. I had failed to make my promised phone call to Toy to tell her of my arrival at Bangkok as my mobile phone started giving me unusual messages, all in Thai, and I had no idea what it was telling me. There was no way now of contacting her. I had, anyway, been a little reluctant to ring her when the plane touched down at Bangkok, as it was then 5.45 in the morning.

It was a relief to be stretching my legs as I walked through the concourse. First stop was the restroom. As I looked into the mirror, I saw an unkempt male, hair uncombed, face unshaven, and with clothes all crumpled. Derek, I thought, you look completely down at heel. I had hoped that my preparations prior to my journey were enough, but the hours of travel had taken its toll. Not only this, but by now the heat of the morning was beginning to make me sweat profusely.

Having selected the best picture of me to send to Toy via the internet, I now had my doubts if she would recognise me from the photo I had sent her.

I had brought over some cheeses from the UK and they were in my hand luggage.

My attempts to blame my body odour on my Camembert and Stilton cut no ice with my fellow travellers. I was sure Toy would also not be fooled. I had to do something very quickly as I only had just a little over one hour before landing at Chiangmai on the final leg of my long journey.

I could do little about my appearance but perhaps a quick visit to the perfume counters in duty free with the numerous testers available might have the desired result of making me more presentable. In the rush to improve my aroma at the perfume stores of duty free, I had not realised that I had been holding my cabin bag all the time in my right hand. Only one side of me had received the many squirts of after-shave that I had tried. I must have smelt like a Parisian brothel as I waited to board the next flight.

I had already given Toy my full flight details, providing her with my flight number and arrival time at Chiangmai international airport. Toy had promised that she would be there to meet me in the arrivals hall. As my flight was on a domestic route within Thailand, all the passengers were bussed out to the much smaller plane that was waiting for us. We had to walk the last hundred yards. I was still amazed that, even over that short stroll, I continued to have sweat dripping off me. Some passengers, mainly Thai, did not seem to mind but a few appeared to be suffering the same discomfort as me.

It was not long before I was drying off in the air-conditioned cabin of this tiny aircraft. Sipping an orange juice and having a light snack, I was trying not to fall asleep. The jet lag was beginning to get to me and I felt very tired. Seeing the city of Bangkok steadily getting smaller as we ascended into the skies, I was struck by just how sprawling a city Bangkok is. Houses, warehouses, and other buildings tightly packed together. Factories billowing smoke and pollution into the atmosphere. The roads were becoming congested; some lines of traffic were clearly at a standstill. This was the early morning rush hour. I was to learn later that Bangkok's rush hour actually lasts all day long! I had a lot to learn about Thailand.

The flight was only an hour long and, as we started to descend into the Northern Province of Chiangmai, a very different vista appeared as I looked out of my window. The buildings were not so close together and there were a lot of green fields. Many were flooded rice paddies sheltered by the more mountainous countryside of the North. The many lakes and winding rivers reflected the bright sunshine back towards the plane making it hard to view what was below. We were gliding across buildings, getting lower and lower until we crossed the boundary of the airport and touched down smoothly on the tarmac, breaking gently until we almost came to a halt as the plane turned right towards the terminal. I marveled at the sight outside my window as
I could clearly see that we had landed in the lee of the mountains and high above me the temple of Doi Suthep was sparkling in the sunlight.

There are splendid views of the city from Doi Suthep provided visibility is not hampered by the pollution of forest fires during the hot season. The temple's most famous shrine is that of the white elephant. Legend has it that part of the Buddha's shoulder bone was placed on the back of a white elephant by the king of the Lanna kingdom, King Noonaone. It was released into the jungle but climbed the mountain of Doi Suthep, trumpeting three times before dying on the spot where the temple is now built.

Phuping palace, a summer residence of the royal family, lies in meticulously kept grounds about four kilometres further up. Because it is sited higher than the temple and it is customary not to put oneself above a Buddha image, it is not that popular with all members of the Thai royal family.

As we neared the terminal, my mind began to race. Was Toy going to be there? Would I recognise her? Would she recognise me? Would we be able to understand each other? I spoke virtually no Thai and her English, though she could just about get by, was not particularly good.
Would I like her and, more importantly, would she like me. Possibly not straightaway, if the reflection of my features in the mirror at Bangkok airport were anything to go by. Was she going to be overcome by the smell of so many different fragrances on my left side? After so many hours of travelling there were too many questions buzzing around in my brain. I began to feel very nervous as I approached the immigration desk. Five minutes and a short walk later and I was reunited with the single case that I had last seen at the check-in counter at Heathrow.

I had just one more hurdle of officialdom to encounter and that was with customs who, surprisingly on this one occasion, did not stop me. Maybe it was the fact that I was unprepared for the Thai weather and looked like a dirty, wet English tramp, and smelt like something coming out of the fragrance department of Harrods or an outside sewer, depending on which side of me you stood. They gave me a wide berth, preferring to stop all the others behind me. A long way behind me as I recall. All seemingly happy for the additional delay.
I knew that it was not too late to turn round, stay in the confines of the airport, change my tickets if need be, and make my way back to the UK. I still had time to change my mind. However, I timidly approached the automatic, frosted glass doors that would lead me to the arrivals concourse where Toy had promised to meet me. She had

booked a hotel for me and had told me before my flight that it was not far from her school or from the airport. Was that a hint that I could run back anytime during my stay? I had the name of the hotel in my wallet so, if she was not waiting at the arrivals area, I could at least enjoy a break seeing the sights alone, if I decided to stay.

Toy was born in a poor farming family many miles from Chiangmai, in a village just outside Tak, quite close to the Burmese border. She was the eldest daughter, having an older brother, and a younger brother and sister. As tradition dictates, it is the eldest daughter who is expected to remain at home to look after the parents in their old age, with the other children contributing financially as much as they can. In Thailand, there is no effective welfare system as enjoyed in the West. It bears no comparison with the English system. Here, it is *no work; no pay*. Looking after sick, infirm, or unemployed relatives is a family not a state responsibility.

When it came to Toy's high school education, her parents held finance back. Their daughter's life had already been mapped out by the conventions that had been followed by many generations before her. Her job was to look after them as they grew older. Toy was determined to break with such customs and she set out to raise money to pay for her own education. She worked on a neighbour's rice farm, as well as looking after water buffalo for other farmers. She made rice sweets to sell at local markets. Much to the annoyance of her parents, Toy, through sheer determination, saved enough money to commence her schooling.

It was near the end of her studies that her mother became terminally ill. And late one night, despite the arguments they had had about her education, Toy held her mother's hand and promised always to take care of the family, in particular her youngest brother, Nok. As she whispered, *"I love you. Sleep now, mother, you need to rest. Don't worry about anything,"* her mother's life started to slip away. They were Toy's last words to her mother. She was just eighteen years old and now had the duty and responsibility of looking after the entire family.

Toy's father remarried just three months after his wife's death. Most unusual, as there are 100 day and one year ceremonies following a death in Thailand. His remarriage caused a certain amount of tension between the father and his youngest son, Nok, with Toy stepping in many times to stop him from beating his son. Nok had turned to drugs and drink. Remembering her promise to her dying mother to take him under her wing. Toy was guiding and encouraging her brother to join either the army or the police force.

Toy married just before her twenty-first birthday and her first and only daughter was born a year later. Somchai was an engineer and after Kanya's birth left home to work for a company in the Middle East. He sent money to his wife from time to time, but not enough to look after the family. Toy had to find extra money from somewhere to provide for her daughter and to fund her teacher-training course. For the second time in her life, she showed she had the strength of mind and resolve to work at anything to achieve her aims. She sold lottery tickets and worked at many mundane jobs. She had little free time. Gambling is illegal but Thai law allows the sale of state lottery tickets, though more usually the sellers are restricted to those with disabilities. Certainly, preference is given to such people as a form of state help for the under-privileged. It is seen as a token gesture in a country where the state does not have strong welfare provision.

Somchai returned from the Middle East a changed man. Much wealthier than he had ever been, Somchai found he had many friends who were more than happy to share his good fortune at some bar or other. Toy at this time had obtained a university degree and started work at a school far from the family home. She was able to return only at weekends to look after her daughter and clean house. Her husband, on the other hand, did no work and enjoyed the single life during the week. I had been told, and at the time believed, that he would go out on the town every night, returning home blind drunk, and often with a different woman to share his bed. Somchai sometimes took his rage out on his daughter, hitting her with a wire clothes hanger. Most nights, Kanya took refuge in her room and kept out of his way.

These events were not fully relayed to Toy on her weekend visits but eventually she began to gain a better picture of what Kanya's life was like when she was not at home. Her lonely existence reminded me of my own unhappy life in my granny quarters back in England. Had I been captivated by Toy's conversations on line? Perhaps I was identifying their hardships and unhappiness with my own. Perhaps I was too ready to accept what appeared to be parallels between our two lives. Walking through the airport, all this was flashing through my mind. I had no reason at the time to doubt what she had been telling me on the internet.

The final straw came, Toy had said, when she caught her husband sleeping with her own sister. She demanded a divorce. The law in Thailand is different from that in the UK and the States. It is difficult to get a divorce here unless both parties agree. Usually a financial inducement, money or land, has to be offered by one party to the other. If the case has to go to court, the judges will always look at ways of possible reconciliation. They, like all Thais, want to avoid conflict at all costs. It is a feature of Thai society. Proceedings can go on for years with stalling tactics being employed at every turn.

This seemed to be the predicament that Toy found herself in. Then the dilemma was solved in a most unanticipated way. The husband's nightly jaunts always ended in his riding home much the worse for drink. Accidents and damage to property became commonplace, with Toy, as the only bread-winner, having to pick up the tab. Cats reputedly only have nine lives, and Somchai's luck was bound to run out sooner or later. On his way home one night, Somchai crashed his motorbike into a female motorcyclist as she was returning from her work at a local factory. Both were killed instantly. At the age of thirty, Toy had become a widow.

Maybe not in this case, but it is not uncommon in Thailand for a husband or wife to claim they are widowed rather than admit to being divorced. It saves social embarrassment and is regarded as a mere white lie, not causing any real harm to anyone. Much the same as when some Thais exaggerate their job position and educational qualifications.

Outside schools and offices, you will often see an organisation chart with photos of each employee. Thais like to show their position in the hierarchy. Vets, for example, will proudly put up their qualifications on their reception wall together with a photo of their receiving their university degree from a member of the royal family.

It was not long before arguments took place with Somchai's family over money. Toy was aware that, completely alone, she was never going to win against his family. She packed her bags and took her daughter to her school lodgings. Having listened to Toy's explanation of her situation, the school authorities agreed to accept Kanya as a pupil in the school and for her to be allowed to live with her.

Thinking of Kanya's long-term future, Toy then decided to move to Chiangmai, where better educational facilities were available for Kanya and where there was a good choice of university level education. There were, however, no boarding facilities available in the school grounds for a teacher with a daughter. She did eventually find a one bed-roomed wooden house in which they could both live. Though very basic at 100 baht a night, it was convenient for both Toy's work and Kanya's school.

Eight years had passed since Somchai had died. Toy and Kanya had now been alone for all that time and were inseparable. There was understandably a strong bond between them. It was this bond and Kanya's wish that she wanted her mother to *"find a new husband for yourself and a father for me. Let's be a family together again,"* that had made me make this 12,000 round trip to see them.

A few more minutes and I would be walking through the door into the arrivals area. We would be meeting each other for the first time face to face.

Or so I thought.

Chapter 3   No Show

There was no one resembling Toy in the arrivals hall. She and Kanya had said they were coming to meet me. Most of the people waiting for friends that had just landed were, as one would expect, Thai. But there were no mother and daughter couples as far as I could see. Perhaps she had been delayed? I had not been able to phone her because I had not been able to get my Thai mobile to work in Bangkok. It would have been impossible for her to let me know.

I decided to wait one hour. If she did not turn up, I would either make my way to the ticketing office and arrange for my return flight or stay alone for a few days in Chiangmai. I could not think straight at the moment. Sitting alone in the arrivals hall, I was heart-broken and confused. I began thinking about what I *actually* knew of this person using an English nickname instead of her Thai name. This was getting a little suspicious. Her family lived near the Burmese border. Were they really Thai? Was *Tasanee* a Thai name? I had no idea. Had she really worked on a neighbour's rice farm, looked after water buffaloes for other farmers, and made rice sweets to sell at local markets to help her get through school and university.

Well, that was what she had told me. Had I been misled by these sob stories just to get me interested in coming to Thailand to see her? Was she genuinely interested in a possible friendship? Or, did she now have cold feet and had no intention of turning up? With those thoughts still in my mind, I glanced at the clock. One hour had passed. I admit that I was almost in tears. A young lad came up to me.

"Can I help you, sir?"
"Not really, I've been waiting for someone for over an hour and she's not turned up."
"Did you come off the Bangkok flight?"
"Yes"
"Knowing the flight has come from Bangkok, she's probably waiting at Domestic Arrivals. People don't realise that passengers with checked-through luggage from abroad are directed to

International Arrivals. It's an easy mistake to make. Happens all the time."

Dragging my cases through the door to the Domestic concourse, I could hear a loud buzz of animated voices. I walked slowly towards the excitement until I was standing behind a small crowd of people, all holding up boards with the names of their expected guests written on them. They all had their backs to me, of course, because they were watching for domestic passengers coming through the domestic door. I was coming from a different part of the airport.

Then I saw them. Two slim Thai ladies with flowing black hair. Toy had sent me photos of herself and her daughter with a full description giving details of their height and weight. Always meticulous, Toy had left nothing to chance. Although a little nervous, I confidently approached from behind, tapped Toy on the shoulder, and said: *"Hello, Toy, surprise, surprise."* I had found them and my worries and doubts of an hour ago were over. They turned towards me and held up the large name card that they were both holding. But my name was not on it. I had been mistaken. The ladies had been waiting for someone else. I quickly apologised. Then I heard my name being called.

"Dee rick, Dee rick." I turned round and saw for the first time the woman who had enthralled me on the internet. The Thai way of pronouncing Derek was the sweetest sound I had ever heard. Well worth traveling 6000 miles to hear. Her tight jeans concealed a slim waist and her hips swayed naturally with every small step she took towards me. Her long black hair cascading over her shoulders, framing her high cheek boned face. Dark piercing eyes and an open smile showing bright white teeth. I was filled with passion as she lowered her head and brought her hands up to her face in the traditional Thai greeting, the *wai*. *"Sawatdee Ka, Dee rick. Welcome to Chiangmai."*

"Good to see you, Toy. I was worried when I first arrived and could not see you. I had been directed to the other arrivals lounge." I could not take my eyes off this Thai goddess or the young lady in a

white blouse and blue skirt who was accompanying her. Kanya smiled happily as she stood behind her mother.

We walked out into the open furnace that is the Thai summer and towards the car park. Her dark green, rather battered, car had been left in the sun and was even hotter than the outside temperature. The air-conditioning was set at full power and Toy ensured all the air vents were aimed in my direction. Sitting in the car on the way to my hotel, I learnt a few unusual features of Thai driving. Toy, indicating left, slowed slightly on approaching a red light but did not stop. She ignored the light and turned left in the direction she wanted to go. What on earth was she doing? It petrified me. She then explained that at most, though not all, lights you can filter left when on red provided that it is safe to do so. Though you need to watch for motorcyclists coming towards you on the wrong side of the road when you filter left.

As we pulled into the Phucome Hotel, two bellboys rushed out and took my luggage to reception, while I, the weary *farang* (the term used by Thais for white foreigners), followed mother and daughter into the foyer.

Although some Thais can sometimes use it discourteously if they are annoyed with someone, visitors should not react with anger if they are called *farang*. In western countries, it is rude and bad practice to use the word foreigner when speaking of a visitor or guest. Here, it is normally regarded as acceptable and no offence is intended. Even though the word for foreigner in Thai is *kon tangchat*, it is virtually never used. Chinese are referred to as *kon cheen* (or *chek*, though that is certainly rude). *Khaek* is the word used for foreigners wearing turbans. Even a nationalised Thai who is a member of a hill-tribe and has a Thai ID will usually be called *chao thai poo kao*
(Thai people from the hills) or simply *chao kao*. The Thai use of words other than *kon tangchat* to describe people they see as not fully Thai does not have the same insulting undertone as in the West. That said, the hill tribe people are sensitive about being called *chao kao* and a Thai would avoid using the term in their presence. So,

despite what the guidebooks may have you believe, *farang* does not refer to all foreigners and is certainly not always bad mannered.

After a few more *wais* from the staff, I signed in and my passport was checked and photocopied a few times. Toy was handed the keys and we went upstairs. The excitement, the journey, and the heat were now beginning to sap whatever energy I had left. Toy opened the door to my third floor room and we went in. Despite it being just ten in the morning, all I could think of was lying on the bed and getting a good rest. Toy must have understood this and suggested that I have a relaxing shower followed by some sleep. She and Kanya would return later.

After my shower, I crashed out on the bed. I awoke a few hours later, got dressed, and began to unpack. Toy had asked for a room at the back of the hotel to avoid the noise of the main road in the front. My room faced the mountains and I had imposing views from both my windows. By leaning out a little, I could see the golden buildings of Doi Suthep, the temple I first saw as I flew into Chiangmai. Looking down on the streets below, I could see people busy with their daily lives. Women hanging their washing out to dry on their balconies. Tall modern buildings and old wooden shacks with tin roofs nestled closely together. I found it amusing that some homes had a garden watering system set up on the roof, and jets of water could be seen like falling rain on the rusting corrugated roofs. A practical attempt to cool the rooms beneath. Toy arrived a little later while I was watching a TV program on the King's recent visit to a hill-tribe project. I understood nothing of what was being said; but could appreciate, from watching the film, just how much the people were grateful for his involvement in their lives. On the journey to the hotel, I had noticed car stickers with the words "*Kao rak nai luang*" (We love our King) on the rear windows. This film reinforced the truth of how well loved the King is in Thailand.

It was lunchtime and I was hungry. Toy and Kanya decided it was time for me to experience my first taste of Thai food. Toy helped by telling me what to eat and what not to eat, and they both laughed at my poor attempts at using chopsticks to eat my noodles. Toy called the waiter over and asked him to give me a spoon and fork. That was much easier. Thais use chopsticks for noodles but a spoon and fork for other meals. Food is already in mouth-sized portions so knives are not necessary. I've never been happy using bits of wood to eat my food anyway.

We returned to the hotel laughing and joking as I practiced my ten-word Thai vocabulary on passers-by. I gave Toy and Kanya the gifts I had brought over from England. We laughed again as we realised they were all made in China. It was three o'clock in the afternoon, so we decided to stroll around the *sois* (alleyways) around the hotel. I was spellbound by the hustle and bustle of the markets and the people eating by the side of the road. Everyone smiling. I find it difficult to describe the laidback and happy atmosphere that was everywhere around me.

I was up unusually early the next day and, armed with my breakfast tokens, went down to the hotel dining room to be greeted by hotel staff dressed in colourful silk outfits that clung tightly to their bodies. The girls as "drop dead gorgeous" as the cabin staff on the plane coming over. It was about six in the morning and I was faced with a wide selection of food ranging from curry, spring rolls, fried fish, squid, to the more comforting sight, at least for my stomach, of boiled eggs, bacon, and toast. There were also high piles of fresh fruits such as watermelon, pineapple, and oranges. There were many others that I did not even recognise. They all looked enticing and mouth-watering. I tried a few. Oh yes, very tasty.

Toy had arranged to meet with me at 10am so I had plenty of time to look around the area. The morning rush hour was well underway with motor bikes jockeying for position in front of the many cars and trucks waiting at the traffic lights. Drivers not wearing seat belts. Motorcyclists, without crash helmets, turning corners or making U-turns without signaling. It was par for the course in Thailand, where driving regulations are not strictly enforced. I learnt later that this was very much to do with the Thai concept of avoiding conflict and taking a more hassle-free approach to life (*mai pen rai* in Thai.) One hand on the handlebar, one hand clutching a mobile phone. A great way to have a conversation while riding. Holding an umbrella or a school textbook over your head to avoid the heat of the sun while riding pillion. Any problem with your female passenger, sitting sidesaddle on the back, drinking an iced coffee with one hand and combing her hair with the other? It is a little dangerous but the Thais never seem to fall off. The riders don't worry; the police don't worry. Life is easier and less stressful if small infringements are disregarded. A Thai driver will sound his horn to warn of his presence. It is common practice. But several loud blasts are totally unacceptable and such anger is not tolerated. Thais dislike confrontation, preferring a tranquil and quiet life.

I walked around in no particular direction and was quite at ease just soaking in the mood of the *soi* people. Street vendors were cooking various meats, the aromas of herbs and spices filled the air. I was no longer hungry after my breakfast, but I was a little tempted by the food I saw on offer. The stalls were all close together and the passageways narrow. As a six-foot Westerner, I was having difficulties avoiding the low-hung shelters and umbrellas that protected the stallholders from the heat of the day. In a few hours, these colorful sunshades would be most welcome. It was still just seven in the morning so I sat myself down at a stall on the side of the road and sipped a drink of iced coffee while watching the world go by. I was enjoying every minute of my first experience of Thai life.

It is sadly going out of fashion now, particularly in the touristy westernised areas and hi-so restaurants; but the Thai custom was always to offer water with every meal. Sitting at a roadside stall, you will be offered a glass of water by the seller. Alternatively, you will be able to help yourself from the water cooler and ice bucket. You pay for the food but the water is complimentary. It's odd, but the most authentic Thai food is better and less expensive at roadside stalls than in posher restaurants. Eateries owned by expats, as well as being more expensive for the same quality of food, tend to sell bottled water rather than follow the Thai custom. They get away with it because they have a captive clientele of English speakers.

I returned to my hotel room and took yet another shower. It was taking time to acclimatise. Before going downstairs to meet Toy, I put on fresh clothes. At this rate, I would run out of newly laundered clothes by the weekend, just two days away. I waited in the relative coolness of the hotel lobby for Toy to arrive. Sitting on a wooden teak chair made to take the weight of an elephant, I picked up some brochures and travel guides to read. I continued browsing as yet another glass of iced water was put in front of me by a waitress in the local Lanna costume. The clock chimed ten and thereafter every quarter of an hour. No sign of Toy. Having drunk nearly eight glasses of water, I had to visit the toilet. I returned to my seat watching the guests arriving and leaving through the entrance of the hotel. Toy arrived just before eleven o'clock.

I was learning something else about Thailand. Appointment times can be approximate. Punctuality, unless essential, does not matter. *Mai pen rai*. The Mexicans have the concept of mañana, meaning that time is not important. The Thais too identify with this idea, but *without* the same sense of urgency! Friends, acquaintances, and even tradesmen may say they are coming tomorrow; when they actually mean some time in the future, if at all.

Thai women take great pride in their appearance and Toy was no exception. I had noticed earlier in the morning how Thai girls rode their motorcycles with their backs up straight, their pillion passenger gracefully balanced sidesaddle on the back. They don't lose their poise even when the rider is careering round bends. Riding pillion is an art form. You can identify foreign tourists who have hired a bike for the first time. The rider is arched over the handlebars, his back is curved, and his passenger is hugging tightly around his waist.

Touching is a delicate question with the Thais. Women must never brush up against or touch a monk. If handing a gift or some food to a monk, she must first place it on a cloth, remove her hand, and allow him to slide the cloth towards him so that he can take the offering. If sitting on a bus with a vacant seat next to her, she should move or swap seats with a man to allow him to sit down and not be next to a woman.

While walking with Toy, I noticed that couples were not holding each other's hands in public as they would in the West. Touching a young child in a friendly way is acceptable but is probably best avoided. Certainly never touch a person's head. It is regarded as a sacred part of the body. In Thailand, the foot is regarded as the lowest and dirtiest part of the body and the head the highest. When Thais sit on the ground, they always point their feet away from others, tucked to the side or behind them. Pointing at or touching something with the foot is considered inappropriate in their culture. A younger person, usually female, may well take your hand when crossing a road if they know you well, though even that is not that common. The best tip is to watch how Thais make contact with one another. It is not generally a "touchy, feely society." Thailand is actually a rather conservative country.

Toy and I spent the day together visiting some of the sights in the centre of Chiangmai. I was learning about Thailand but, more importantly, I was getting to know this lady, who, unlike all the other couples around us, was holding my hand tightly in hers as we went from one tourist attraction to another. There were temples wherever you looked. Each one had something special to offer the visitor. Whether walking the streets, riding in *tuk tuks*, or as pillion passengers on motor cycles, monks in their saffron robes could be seen everywhere.

Over dinner, Toy asked me if I wanted to visit her school the next day. It was an invitation that I accepted gladly as I knew my time in Thailand was limited and I wanted to be with her for as long as possible. It was nearing ten at night when we returned to the hotel foyer to say goodnight. She told me she would return soon.

For the first time in years, I felt myself full of happiness and totally at ease with life. I virtually floated back to my room, knowing Toy would come back in the morning. She was beginning to take control of my life.

Chapter 4   A Thai Thief

I had crammed a lot into my first five days in Thailand. I had been puzzled and perhaps confused by some of the differences I noticed between Thai and western ways. Although the people seemed happy and relaxed, maybe there was something being concealed behind the smile that was on everyone's face. They smiled when there seemed to be nothing to smile about. They smiled when they hit a problem and just walked away. It was hard to understand. I experienced first-hand that Thais would always tell you what they thought you wanted to hear rather than just answering your question.

Not only could it be misleading but also it was a shock to the system. It was *"culture shock."* It is tricky to explain unless you have personally felt it. You can become tired and a little uneasy from the frustrations that these cultural differences cause.

I think jet lag must have been catching up with me. It was 9am and I felt dead tired. Toy must have been reading my mind when she came out of the shower, telling me to rest a little longer and she would return later. I stayed in bed as she kissed my forehead and left the room promising to return later. I must have dozed for an hour or two and it was the hunger pains that persuaded me to get up. I opened the wardrobe doors and, to my horror, found that my suitcase was missing, together with almost all my clothes. I was left with only one shirt and a pair of slacks.
I had been burgled. Nobody would question someone in a hotel walking around wheeling a suitcase, would they?

I checked the bedside drawer. My wallet, air ticket, and passport were inside untouched. No money had been taken. The souvenirs I had bought were still on the table. Only my case of clothes was missing. I got dressed, and went down to reception to report the theft. After a late breakfast, I stayed in the hotel. There would be no point venturing out to continue my exploration of the neighbourhood as I had no fresh clothes. I switched on the TV, hoping that this might take my mind off my predicament.

The door opened. And there was Toy, my suitcase in her hand. Had the hotel staff found it and handed it to her to bring it up to me? With a disarming smile, she told me that she had returned to my room when I was sleeping, taken all the clothes away, including hers, washed them, and put them out to dry.

"I have signed off school for the day. Let's get the ironing done. The rest of the day can be ours." There were more of Toy's clothes than mine. I laughed out loud. Nothing changes when it comes to sharing your wardrobe with a woman. The old iron she was using kept cutting out, taking the creases out of our clothes was going to be a slow process.

That day we spent some time just outside Chiangmai at a beautiful waterfall. Climbing up the rocks, I felt young and mischievous again, the cool spring water running over my feet. I scooped some water in my hands and splashed it over the Thai companion who stood below me. We were both laughing like a couple of young children, playing together without any worries about getting their clothes soaking wet. There were young Thai couples around us who were laughing at how we were enjoying ourselves. However, they seemed more staid and inhibited, not wanting, I suppose, to show their emotions in public. That is a noticeable trait for most Thais.

This was a lady I was slowly falling in love with, bewitched by her subtle charms and even subtler ways of getting me to do what she wanted. However, I had a return ticket to the UK in my wallet, a job to return to when I was fitter for work, and the problem of selling the house. I longed for a permanent relationship with Toy. For the moment, it seemed out of the question.
We dried ourselves as best we could and jumped in the car to do some more sightseeing. The hot water springs, the wood carving village, and the umbrella village at Borsang, made famous by Princess Diana on her first visit to Thailand. We saw the colourful umbrella they made in her honour. It is mentioned in the *Guinness Book of Records* as the largest umbrella ever made.

In the evening, we met up with Kanya and went shopping. I choose a moment when I was alone with Toy's daughter to ask her what her mum would like for her birthday. All she would say was *"Tam jai Dee-rick. It's up to you."* I pointed to some clothes, *"Tam jai Dee-rick"*; there was some jewelry on display, *"Tam jai Dee-rick"* A new telephone? *Tam jai Dee-rick"*

Although I had no idea what Toy might want, I was learning something else about the Thais. They do not like to force their opinions on you and are reluctant to suggest what you should do. That was all very well, but I really did want some suggestions. Nevertheless, that is not the Thai style. To get what they want, they use an intermediary or drop subtle hints at precisely the right moment. It usually works!

All I was getting was "up to you." A year later, with a little more experience, I grasped the reality of her strategy: keep saying, "up to you" until the guy is actually doing what you really wanted anyway.

The next day, while Toy was out of the school's staff room, I explained my plans for her fortieth birthday to two of her colleagues. Mali agreed to get the cake, Pakpao was roped in to get balloons, and my task was to get in touch with Kanya. I swore her to secrecy. I wanted her mum's party tomorrow to be a big surprise. The next day, I was awake before Toy. Without a sound, I put my birthday card on her pillow and a large parcel at the foot of our bed. The noise of the boiling kettle made Toy stir. Wishing her a happy birthday as she opened her card and present, I waited for her reaction. Excitedly, she opened the box. A brand new steam iron. Not the most romantic of gifts but at least she would be able to iron clothes quicker in the future!

Normally, you will find that Thais will not open a gift in front of you. They will smile, thank you, and put it one side to open when they are alone. Westerners find that strange, even rude. Thais do not want to risk showing any disappointment in your choice of gift. They must preserve "face."

A shout came from the bathroom. The whole hotel would have heard it. "What's this?"

I had tied a small bag to the showerhead. I told her to bring it out of the shower. "Happy Birthday, now open it." I think she saw now that this was her real present. A gold necklace with a heart-shaped gem. She moved to the mirror for a better view. Nobody had ever given her a gift like that before. She burst into tears.

After breakfast, we made our way to school. Signing in as usual, Toy took her seat and started preparing her day. Toy's daughter and her colleagues crept in from a rear door singing, "Happy birthday" as they walked towards her. Her friends admired the gold chain around her neck before leading her to another part of the staff room where they had decorated a desk with balloons and flowers. In one corner, they had lightheartedly put up a balloon shaped as a condom. Thais love to make an occasion a fun event. Some parents and children had popped in, many bringing gifts of fruit. A feature of Thai life-style is that people join in at parties. In the towns and cities, one often sees red balloons hung outside bars as a sign that some celebration or other is in progress. Passers-by regularly participate. Thailand is an exceptionally "community" based society.

Thais live as part of their family and as part of their community. They don't live as individuals as we tend to do in the West. When children get their first job, they usually stay with mum and dad even after they get married. Possibly in a small house in the family garden or sometimes in a house nearby. If they have to work away, they will rent a one-roomed apartment but home will still be where the parents are. Always on the telephone and always attending family events.

Mali and Pakpao brought in a birthday cake with its forty small candles. It took Toy two attempts to blow them all out. The next hour or so passed with lots of joking, teasing, singing, and high spirits. Toy had a tear in her eye when she confided in me later that she had never had a party like that before. Her family had been too poor.

It seemed like longer, but Toy and I had been together for only 9 days. Were we going too fast? Was I going too fast? Did I know enough about her after such a short time?

Chapter 5   No Words Spoken

I was pleased that Toy's party had gone so well. I thought that the tear in her eye showed so much more than words could convey. In two days' time I would be boarding a plane back to England. I was going to find it hard to leave her after such an enjoyable time together. Was this going to be just a holiday romance, soon to be forgotten? I hoped not. Was it fair on Toy for us to get so involved when I had yet to sort out the sale of the house in England? Without that sale, I would not be able to return to Thailand or to Toy. That was going to be difficult for both of us to come to terms with.

I had become drunk on the national culture, the sun, the food, and the people. Toy had shown so much love and care towards me. I had been so heartless in my first days to doubt her. I was facing a reality check. Would I see her again once this holiday was over? I wanted time to stop and think. I needed to sort my life out; and I wanted that life to include Toy. It all depended on the house sale. I could not get away from that. Toy saw the problem as clearly as I did. To distract ourselves from the emotions we were feeling, we paid a visit to Mali's half-built home and spent some time at Pakpao's house warming. There were so many of her friends there that it became more of a farewell bash for me than anything else.

Or perhaps I was mistaking typical Thai friendliness and thinking too much that I was the centre of attention. Thais make *farangs* feel important at weddings, and indeed funerals. It does not take anything away from the actual event itself.

There was a distinct silence on the final morning, neither of us wishing to acknowledge that the day of my leaving had arrived. To reassure Toy, I handed her some clothes, saying I will not need these in the UK but will need them when I return. Looking into her eyes, I could see that this small gesture comforted her. Without saying a word to each other, we sat quietly as we journeyed to the airport. After checking in my luggage, we made our way to the departure lounge hand in hand. Kanya and two of her friends were waiting to see me off. It was a nice thought and meant that Toy would not be alone on leaving the airport.

I am not very good at leave-taking. I quickly kissed Toy and assured her that I would return. I did not know whether she believed me or not. Were my words empty of meaning? On later reflection, I think her female intuition would have picked up how I felt about her, and told her that she had already secured what Kanya had referred to as "*a new husband for yourself and a father for me.*"

Toy, Kanya, and her friends gave me the traditional *wai* and I walked briskly through the gate to departures. With just one quick glance over my shoulder and a wave to the lady I knew I was going to miss dearly, I walked out of their view. Was I also walking out of their lives? At the time, I thought that was a possibility. In less than twenty minutes, I was high over the Thai countryside, and in just over two hours, I was on my connecting flight back to London and an uncertain future.

I recalled over and over again the little things that Toy had done to make my trip so enjoyable and relaxing. Setting the air conditioning vents in the car in my direction, the laundering of my clothes, making sure I was always in the shade, ensuring my glass was full of water at all times and much more. I slept during most of the flight and my dreams were of Toy and Thailand.

After a stressful trek through Heathrow airport, and an uncomfortable journey across the London underground, I eventually boarded the train for Sussex. On arriving home, I opened the door to my room and fell exhausted into an armchair. Ignoring the mountain of mail that was waiting for me, I made myself a cup of tea and sent a text to Toy to say I had got home safely.
I could not help thinking about my journey from London to the South Coast and comparing it to my time in Thailand. My first day exploring the *sois* around my hotel, stumbling and tripping over the brightly painted umbrellas of the street vendors, and the smiles and laughter from those around me. The exasperation and commotion at Heathrow was a vivid contrast. No smiles, no helpful responses if you were lost or needed help. There seemed to be lots of people

complaining but getting nowhere; very different from Thailand's more care-free and helpful attitude.

It is true that I had returned to the UK totally refreshed, relaxed and more confident, but the nagging question was why did I feel so different? When comparing the western way and the Thai way my first impressions were that Thais appear to have a more stress free life style and take life less seriously than we do. Was this different outlook on life having such an influence on me?

It was not long before I met my ex-wife in the garden. She came at me with an outburst of very coarse language. I took a lesson from the Thais: I smiled and walked away. From now on, I was going to avoid conflict. I was due to see my doctor a few days after returning from abroad. After examining me he seemed pleased that the medications he had given me had worked so well. He said I seemed much less stressed and more relaxed than he had ever seen me. Yes, he was pleased that the medication he had prescribed had been so successful.

Medications, medications? I tried to hold back a smile. I had not taken one single tablet during my whole time in Thailand with Toy. I had no need of his prescriptions. I had returned to the UK with the same number of pills that I had packed in my case when I left.

He was about to sign me off as fit to return to work, when he suggested he take my pulse and listen to my chest. All was not well and he made me take an ECG to check out my heart. I left the surgery with an appointment card to see a specialist at the first available opportunity.

I was in daily contact with Toy but wondered whether I should tell her of this new development or not? There was still no news on the house sale.

Chapter 6   Talking to My Son

My hospital appointment came more quickly than I had expected.
Hooked up to several machines by what seemed like an endless flow
of wires, I spent two hours on a bed while examinations on my heart
were completed. The good news was that the hospital had found
nothing out of the ordinary. My doctor took me off the sick list. I
was free to go back to work.

I went around to see my son, Michael. I had missed him terribly
and I wanted him to stay a part of my life, however difficult that
might be with his mother discouraging him from seeing me. He
seemed delighted with the gifts and clothes I had brought back for
him, and I proudly showed him all the pictures I had taken in
Thailand, in particular the photos of Toy and myself visiting the
usual tourist spots. Although the elephant football match was of
interest, what surprised him was that elephants could still be seen
walking the streets with their mahouts as in the old days.
He found the photos of the show at the snake farm extremely
fascinating and thought the spectacle looked quite dangerous. We sat
for what seemed like hours talking about Thailand with my showing
him a map and explaining all I had learned and loved about the
country and Toy. I can't remember asking him about the things he
had been doing. There was so much to tell him about Thailand.

He must have relayed much of our conversation to his mother as
she got in the habit of referring to Toy as my *Thai whore*. We were
divorced and I had met Toy only after the decree absolute. What on
earth was her problem?

I started working just three days a week at the bank, but by the
end of the first month I was working my normal hours. Even though
I had been off work for several months, I still retained my full
holiday entitlement, and it was not long before I was planning my
next trip to Thailand to keep my promise to Toy. My airline tickets
were booked for an outward flight one Sunday morning in July. I
had to start thinking of how I was to get to the airport for the start of
my twelve day vacation. Heathrow is not my favourite place to board

a plane and start a holiday; getting from the car park to the terminal building and eventual departure gate can be a nightmarish experience.

Then a misfortune turned into a piece of luck. My car had been involved in a rear end collision. A 40-ton lorry having run into me when it failed to stop at some red lights. The repair would take at least a week. I arranged for the garage to pick me up, drop me at airport departures, and collect me on my return. Perfect. The ex-wife need not know, indeed it would confuse her seeing neither the car in the drive nor me in the garden.

Toy met me at the airport, this time at the right arrivals gate. Instead of taking me to a hotel, she took me straight to her home. Kanya had started university and was therefore living on campus. Not having been to Toy's room before, I was a bit shocked to see how very basic it was.
She rented a small unit in a large block of similar sized apartments. There was one large room, a Thai-style toilet and shower, an open-air kitchen, and a small balcony where her pet rabbit, Brown, lived. The main room in many Thai homes is where they both eat and sleep. Although most of the time they will eat outside, chatting and socialising with the neighbours. Having separate bedrooms, whilst becoming more popular, is unusual in poorer areas. When it is time to sleep, you pull down a mattress and lay it on the floor.

The day after my arrival I left with Toy to go to school. Toy's friends once again greeted me, but this time I felt a little more warmth in the welcome, and I am sure this was not due to the many biscuits, sweets and chocolate treats I had brought with me for them to enjoy. While Toy was teaching, I stayed in the staff room answering the endless questions being fired at me. It was good to see Pakpao again. She had returned to her normal shape having given birth to a healthy boy, nicknamed Atom. In everyday conversation, Thais use nicknames. Their real names being used only on formal occasions and for official documents. I could never get my tongue around their full names anyway. Nicknames are sometimes given in celebration of a birth. One of Toy's colleagues, who had had difficulty in conceiving, named her first child *Kawpkhun*, "thank you" in Thai. Her second child was "Green Grass" and the third was nicknamed "Third". The family had obviously run out of new ideas for nicknames.

Other names I have come across are Coco, Cookie, First, *Oi*, (sugar cane), *Nung*, (the number one), Boss, Mine, and my favourite, Cartoon. The Thais love using English words as nicknames. Sometimes, Thais may have more than one nickname; one used by the family, the other used by friends. I had often heard Toy call one of her teacher friends *Pee* Wilai when her name was actually Wilai. The *Pee* in front of a name denotes an elder brother or sister and is used as a form of respect even when you are not related. I still make the mistake of calling her *Pee* Wilai though I should not do so as she is younger than me.

It can be insulting for a Thai to be called *Pee* by an older person, but most Thais appreciate that no disrespect is meant when used by a foreigner. Thais are very accommodating of mistakes made by *farangs*. They don't mind. *Mai pen rai*, yet again.

Surnames in Thailand have only been used since 1913 and should you come across two people with the same surname you can be fairly sure that they are related, however distantly. King Rama VI made it a condition that Chinese wanting to become Thai citizens had to take a Thai surname. Thais who have a hill tribe background can have difficulties registering surnames.

That night Toy and I went for a meal and chatted endlessly under the stars, but I had no good news for her with regard to my situation back in the UK. It was as if life was standing still for both of us. I was unsure if Toy was going to be prepared to wait. I clearly could not continue flying out to Thailand every three months or so for a few days of happiness together. This too had been recognised already by many of her friends back at school. She confided in me that some of her friends had said that they did not expect to see me again after I had returned to the UK in March. I reassured Toy that my intentions were honourable but I could not allow her to wait indefinitely. My life was on hold and I did not want Toy to share in this uncertainty.

I spent many a happy hour attending school and took a close interest in the daily routine. Every day at 8am, the children stand and sing the national anthem. On Fridays, they wear their traditional costumes. Each hill tribe has its own distinctive and colourful dress, while children from the nearby villages and towns are dressed in Lanna style.

Many major companies and local government departments regularly approach the school with requests for the children to be photographed or take part in promotional activities. A win-win situation. The school obtains a fee, the students get a little pocket money, and the corporations get valuable advertising for their products.

Toy wanted me to meet her family in Tak, so we set out early one Saturday morning for the three-hour journey to her father's home. Driving up into the mountains, we passed many trucks filled to over-flowing with goods of all descriptions. It is not unusual to see a crate of chickens or other livestock fall off as a lorry careers around a tight bend, and for the driver to have to stop, round up his flock, and try to re-secure the load. Twice we saw buses parked on the verges with steam coming out of their radiators after overheating. The passengers taking advantage of the break by having an improvised picnic on the side of the road. They all looked very happy.

We pressed on, being careful to avoid any deer that may be emerging unexpectedly from the forest. Once we had cleared the mountain roads and were approaching Tak, we stopped at a small café for a bite to eat and to buy some food to take to her father. Toy ordered several meals which were put in small plastic bags tied with a rubber band. There are always plenty of food and fruit stalls on the side of the road in this country. You need never starve on a long journey. It is also customary in Thailand to ask for any food you cannot finish to be put in a bag to take-away.

One hour later, having passed a few road-side counters selling kitchen knives, a nursery of garden plants, a small drug store, and a few more noodle stalls; we turned into a compound of four metal-roofed houses on stilts. Her father lived in one house; relatives, some quite distant, in the others. Toy reversed into a shady area under some trees and we got out of the car into the midday heat. Always a shock to the system for many *farangs*. Toy had not told her father that we were paying him a visit.

I was surprised to see so many smiling faces sitting around low bamboo tables, chatting, preparing food, or hand washing laundry. Children were playing in the yard, tiny infants were asleep in hammocks, babies were wrapped in a shawl around their mothers' bodies, and chickens were roaming free, picking up scraps of rice from the ground.

Toy unpacked the car and started to hand out sweets to the children who had gathered round. Some she knew, most she did not. Toy's father came down the steps of his home pulling on a clean white vest as he approached. His new wife following, wearing a long skirt right down to her ankles and a brightly coloured shirt. Toy *wai'd* her father and his wife. As they were older than me, I also *wai'd* them. We all sat together in a spot out of the sun and heat, drinking the refreshing iced water which is always quickly brought out to guests whenever someone visits a Thai home.

Toy never looked her father straight in the eye, and the conversation seemed very stiff and formal, totally lacking in affection. Her Dad never looked directly at her and seemed ill at ease. She occasionally interpreted what was being said, but I was mostly in the dark about the conversation. My Thai vocabulary was very limited – just a dozen words or so.

Despite the galvanized roof, the house seemed relatively cool. The inside of this teak home was dark with few windows. There was one main room with two very small bedrooms leading off. Both had just mattresses on the floor and mosquito nets hanging from the ceiling. Some clothes were stacked on shelves, while others hung from an open rail. On the walls of the main room hung pictures of his family, and a picture of the King, Rama IX, taken from an old calendar. Hundreds of thousands of homes in Thailand are exactly like this. Apart from a few wooden chairs, there is little furniture. An old fridge in the corner and a small TV on a makeshift trestle. Eating takes place either on the floor or outside. No aircon of course, and only the occasional fan. Electric wiring dangling loosely from the ceiling and insecurely fixed to the walls. No earth or other safety devices. Most tourists don't get to see how the ordinary Thai lives.

I saw for the very first time a black and white photo of Toy's mother taken just before she died and one of her father as a young man. There was a picture of Toy receiving her degree from a member of the royal family and another of Toy's younger brother in the army. There were no photos of her elder brother or younger sister. He did not live on the compound and rarely visited his father; she had married against her father's wishes and was seen as the black sheep of the family.

Visiting this village was like going back several decades. Some of the women were looking after the children and the elderly; while the younger women and the men were working in the rice paddies. Long hours, bent double, but pacing themselves as they work in the hot sun. They chatted, joked, and sometimes burst into song. Every so often a child or an older person would come round with a jug of water and a ladle, and pour out some water for each worker.

I did not realise then, but I understand better now, the significance of a woman taking a man to see her parents and family. It is not so much to get approval – though a dowry will be negotiated later if a marriage takes place – but to state publicly that the man is more than just a casual friend. It shows that the woman sees the relationship as one she regards as permanent.
If a man does not intend the friendship to develop so quickly into an engagement or a wedding, he should not accept an invitation to the family home. The visit signals a future wedding. Not going at least saves any face being lost. Thai men are conscious of these protocols. I was not. And Toy had not enlightened me.

We had been two hours at her father's home, a short time but long enough for Toy. We said our goodbyes and went on the second leg of our journey to visit Toy's aunt and cousins. Toy had often stayed at her home as a young girl whenever there were disputes at home over her education and ambitions. The reception from her aunt's family was warmer and friendlier than at her father's. Toy was noticeably relaxed and appeared to enjoy catching up on the local gossip and reminiscing about the old days.

The years of suffering and hard work in the fields showed plainly on the faces of her aunt and uncle, now wrinkled after a lifetime in the hot sun. Older than Toy's father, they had difficulty in walking upright and had to use a stick to get about. Their children, grandchildren, and great grandchildren were gathered around playing, laughing, and enjoying their simple happy life. They were a typically close-knit Thai family, totally supportive of one another, with strong bonds amongst themselves and the local community. The journey home took less time as we did not need to stop to eat. Toy's duty done for another year.

Chapter 7 Feeding the Cat

I woke early on Sunday leaving Toy asleep for as long as possible. I knew there was no respite in her working. She was due back at school by 9 am. As a boarding school, at least two members of staff need to be on duty at any one time.

I was left alone all morning and for the first time I was able to visualise Toy's life with
Kanya. The accommodation was basic, but Toy had made it a home to bring up her daughter. Yes, it needed a new coat of paint, and perhaps some modern furniture, but it was more than adequate as it was essentially only a place to sleep. Toy's computer remained in the corner, the same computer that she and Kanya must have sat at for hours on end when sending me messages when I was in England and surfing the net.

Books and papers from school were piled nearby and shoes still in their boxes were stacked neatly by the metal door that led outside. In front of the bed stood a cabinet on top of which rested the television. I saw in my mind both Toy and Kanya laying in bed at night watching the latest Thai soap before dropping off to sleep. A double wardrobe, heaving under the weight of clothes, was one side of the TV. On the other side there stood a set of drawers. Beside the computer were a two-piece suite and a single small chair. But they were used to store even more books and papers. No room to sit on them. Thais are great hoarders.

The room was obviously comfortable for both Toy and Kanya and far better than that enjoyed by Toy's father back in Tak. I suppose Westerners would not be comfortable living there. It lacked the facilities foreigners have come to expect, and living with intermittent water, internet, and electricity supplies annoys many *farangs* living in Thailand.

My thoughts were interrupted by a scratching sound coming from the small balcony. Getting up to investigate, I opened the door to witness Brown, the pet rabbit, standing there with his plastic bowl in his mouth waiting to be fed. I gave him some food, poured myself a coffee, and watched the world go by outside. A young father dressed only in shorts and vest was walking around cradling a young child in his arms. Mothers were riding off on their motorbikes, often with a child or two on the pillion seat, to get food from the local market. Washing was being hung out to dry on the balconies across the way. Police officers with side arms were preparing for work. It was a tranquil scene with no one seeming to be in much of a hurry.

Toy's home was close to Chiangmai's sports complex, named *Jet Roi Pee*, built in the 1990s to host the Asian games and to commemorate Chiangmai's 700 years as a Lanna city. The stadium has an impressive range of amenities including swimming pools, athletics circuits, and tennis and basketball courts. It is very popular with the locals. You will see joggers and cyclists taking full advantage of the facilities particularly in the early morning and late evening. Thais are very much into fitness regimes. Out of town, it is quite common to see walkers and runners dodging the traffic and motor cycles on the busy *sois*.

This was only my second trip to Thailand and with the benefit of hindsight, I could see that both Toy and I were having our futures planned and mapped out by friends and acquaintances here in Chiangmai. Toy's colleagues from school were seeing us as a couple, an item. Invitations to parties and social events came regularly during this second visit, as I was seemingly being groomed to Thai life. A life that I was enjoying but one that I could not commit myself to due to the uncertainties of my life back in the UK.

My twelve days flashed passed and I was soon standing in the departure lounge at Chiangmai airport, Toy next to me. Her eyes were red from crying as, unlike my last farewell, she was alone. I wanted to stay to comfort her, to reassure her that we will be together again soon, but I could not give her false hopes and certainly could not make any promises to her that I may have to break.

"Be strong," I said, and making one promise I knew I could easily keep, "I'll contact you every day."

Chapter 8   Problems at Work

Targets, targets, targets. I was being pressured by my employers to go for more business even though it was clearly not in the best interests of the bank's customers. Work, previously done by colleagues now made redundant, was increasingly being passed to me. The bosses were playing a nasty little game with most of my office colleagues, but the prime focus seemed to be on me. My doctor had put me back on medication for stress and my ex-wife was continually taunting me about my Thai whore. Rarely was I able to see Michael though I did keep my promise to get in touch with Toy each day. At least that was something positive which helped to maintain my sanity. I didn't tell her about the problems at work or the non-stop abuse from my ex, but I think she realised all was not well. A woman's intuition I suppose.

I had booked another flight to Thailand for 17 December. I was not going to have another sad UK Christmas. I tried not to let the stress of the remaining days before the flight get to me. On the plane, I had forgotten to turn off my cell phone. It rang loudly. My solicitor was ringing to tell me a buyer had been found and wanted to exchange contracts before the end of December. With the Christmas break coming up, that was obviously a pipe dream. I could not, anyway, get off the aircraft and sign any documents. It could wait until the first week in January. My former wife had apparently agreed to the price at the last minute. It was very good news. I would tell Toy when we met but would also emphasise that things could well go pear-shaped at the last minute. I didn't want her hopes dashed.

Toy and I provisionally started to look for houses to buy. It was quite enjoyable, even exciting, to tour the *moobaans* and compare the different styles of housing available. We did not look at any houses that were not in these gated communities, as Toy had said that most foreigners seemed happier to live where there was some security on hand (often 24/7) and where there were western style facilities such as a clubhouse and communal swimming pool. I had not spoken to any *farangs* but she was probably right.

I knew you could not own land outright in Thailand and that setting up a limited company, though a possible legal way of circumventing the rules for individuals, was also fraught with problems. While it was sometimes acceptable to the land office, using a company to own your home rather than to run a legitimate business for profit, was often queried by the Thai revenue department. As you still had to have 51% of your shareholders as Thais anyway, it did not seem sensible to pursue that route.

It is always difficult for Westerners to accept that they do not own or control the home in which they live. It would never be their decision if they wanted to sell or move house. Some take a pragmatic view and pretend that there will never be any trouble. Sometimes they are right, sometimes the problems can be life changing. It's usually the wife's family rather than the wife that plants ideas into her head about how she can do what she likes with her own property.

Toy said that many expats took a 30 year lease from their wives, whose name the property was in, or had a *usufruct* which provided security of tenure for a period of time, normally 30 years or life. Some lawyers had recommended taking out a "30+30 lease" where the Thai wife would extend the lease for a further 30 years. But that has never been tested in court and there is no specific statute that mentions the legality of such an arrangement.

Completion had not taken place yet on the house in Sussex, so the question of buying a home for ourselves was academic and did not have to be made now. I could put it at the back of my mind for the moment. Toy was not keen to rent. Her home with Somchai had been rented but it is every Thai's dream to own land and a house. If there are children in a marriage the parents will strive to ensure that there is enough money and land available for them to build their own homes when they themselves get married. Not all families can realise that wish but they all have that desire. I could see that Toy would feel more secure if we eventually owned a house together. (Perhaps together should be in inverted commas – it would always be in her name.) It would be Kwang's inheritance when we had both passed on. There was logic in Toy's thinking and I accepted it.

I knew too that it would be difficult for Toy to explain why, having married a *farang*, she was living in rented accommodation instead of owning land and a house. We continued to look at houses while we did the usual tourist attractions and spent some time with Toy's friends. I was still in love with Thailand and this Thai lady was becoming very much part of my life. I thought we could have a good life together. It would not be that different from living in the West. I could adapt to the way Thais live. We are all human beings; they aren't that different from us. Cultural problems were, I thought at the time, being exaggerated. I could handle it.

I enjoyed my Christmas break in Thailand. I could not see myself ever being in the UK over Christmas again. My mind was continually on the house sale, I could not block it out, but neither did I want to discuss it with Toy. Although it probably wasn't a good idea to bottle up the worry and stress inside me, I did not want her to share my concerns.

I spent a lot of time at Toy's school, correcting some of the English translations the teachers had drafted for their school promotions. I even tidied up the English in a document that the school had to send to Bangkok. I was happy to help but would have liked to have seen more efforts from the education ministry in Bangkok in improving teachers' overall command of the English language. That was not a problem unique to Toy's school. National resources are limited and there are fewer foreign nationals teaching in the schools and universities than in other countries in the Asean group. Where foreigners are employed, the standards are not always that high and one wonders if qualifications are ever checked. Many of the other countries in Asean pay foreign teachers more than those in Thailand and thus attract the better teacher.

In order of GDP (gross domestic product, an economic indicator of a country's wealth), the IMF has ranked each Asean country, giving the highest first. Singapore, Brunei, South Korea, Malaysia,

Thailand, Indonesia, Philippines, Vietnam, Laos, Cambodia, and Burma. Thailand's GDP is 16% of that for Singapore.

Some backpackers and expats teach informally despite not having any English language or teaching qualifications and experience. Some are extremely competent, and have a natural aptitude for teaching, most have limited English skills themselves. Being able to speak colloquial English should not be a passport to teaching English as a foreign language. I recognised that, with limited resources, Thai schools were forced to accept this largely free resource. One solution may be to take advantage of the large number of long-term tourists and expats by encouraging them to improve Thai national teachers' conversational and pronunciation skills by arranging workshops where the Thai teachers and English native speakers could get together. That would work if there was control over the selection and it was reinforced by an improved grammar syllabus in teacher training colleges. It does in the Philippines.

Apart from my time in the schoolroom, I spent every other waking minute with Toy visiting places in and near Chiangmai. Most of them I had been to before but the buzz and atmosphere of being around ordinary Thais still held a fascination for me. I wandered around the noisy and crowded street markets with their colourful stalls, stopped to taste the aromatic and freshly cooked snacks on offer. This life style was so unlike that of the West. And I realised I was falling for it. With the exception of breakfast, we seldom had a meal at home as Toy preferred to go out for meals. Before she met me it would have been most likely at a roadside stall similar to those I had myself discovered. This is where most Thais eat and the staple food is either boiled rice, fried rice, or noodles. Green vegetables are often served free as a side dish together with a weak soup made from the boiling water used to cook the meat dish. Chicken and pork are the favourites but you get only a few slices on top of your rice. A far cry from the "meat and two veg" I had come to expect in England.

It is the way the Thais have always eaten; little and often. No problem for them as from very early morning there are always food shops open by the side of the road and in all the markets. After meeting me, though, Toy acquired a fondness for the more up-market Thai restaurants where there was a greater variety of meats and fishes on offer. Often the meals were plated for each individual –western style – instead of bowls being placed in the middle of the table for everyone to serve themselves. I was used to that style of eating and appreciated being in an air conditioned room. It was really Toy that made the move to that style of eating, even though she had never grown up to it. Many Thais, usually when they are with *farangs* prefer to be seen in what some may regard as "hi-so" establishments. In reality, apart from the appeal of a wider choice of food, they do not represent good value for money and are nowhere near as delicious and fresh.

On the other hand, I did meet some other expats at these restaurants and cafés. It was comforting to have a conversation in English occasionally. My Thai had not got any better and I knew I would never be able to master the language or get by in it. I relied on Thais being able to understand my English or on Toy doing all the translating for me. Initially, I was annoyed with myself for not making a better attempt to learn Thai and communicate with the locals in their own language, but, on talking with other expats, I learnt that they had not bothered to learn Thai and were relying on their wives and partners in communicating with Thais. If they could survive here without knowing the language, I saw no reason why I could not do so.

Even many of those that had been determined to get to grips with the language of the country they were now permanently living in had given up after a few months. Thai is a tonal language and how you pronounce a word can alter its meaning. *Ma*, pronounced in different ways, can mean horse, dog, and come. *Kao* has four meanings: fishy, news, rice, and white. They are written differently in Thai script and that makes them easier to distinguish and is a good guide to how to pronounce the word. But when written in English characters they are spelt the same. There is no one official way for a Thai word to be written using the English alphabet.

I went along to a local expats club to try to widen the number of people I knew; I was conscious that all my acquaintances were mainly Toy's work colleagues. It would, I thought, be vital for me to have a wider social circle to include both Thai and *farang* friends. The set-up did not really appeal to me though. There seemed to be a little bitchiness against Thais in general, always finding fault and criticising at every opportunity. And there was always some expat hovering around trying to rent you a condo or sell you insurance. I felt uneasy and knew that that was not for me. I wanted to integrate and have a mix of Thai and foreign friends, but not in such an artificial commercial environment. If I settled here, I would have to work on integrating. I was sure Toy would help me fit in when, with a bit of luck, I was able to make my final move to the land of my dreams.

I was in love with Toy. She had showed she wanted to care for me and she was clearly motivated to our becoming a happy family together. Just me, Toy, and Kwang. Being secure is key to a Thai's thinking. There is little in the way of a welfare state and the class system, the hierarchy, can be tough for some if they are not born in the right family or do not have the right contacts. Most Thais are content with their lot, unable to change their position in life. They seek security in the family group and in the community. Career progression hardly ever depends on merit. Thailand is a money society and upward mobility is achieved more by using money than any other means.

Opportunities are not readily available for Thais, however ambitious they may be. I could see why so many choose to have a relationship with a *farang*. A better standard of living and a guaranteed financial future.

Chapter 9　I Never Looked Back

I left Thailand the day after New Year's Day, having enjoyed a western style dinner and dance in one of Chiangmai's hotels. Many expats were there but we did not mingle with them. The food was expensive but of high quality and the wide range of Thai and western dishes meant that both Toy and I could eat exactly what we wanted. Meals over the festive season seldom offer value for money anywhere in the world. Here in Thailand, it's an opportunity for restaurateurs, Thai and *farang*, to make a real killing as they can pay their staff their normal wages, holiday premiums not applying in this country even on New Year's Eve. Low labour costs do not translate into lower prices.

Thai businesses historically work on higher gross margins than those in the West. Overall, prices may appear lower because Thailand is a low wage economy. In judging a price, always remember that the average wage is 300 baht a day. That stimulates you to put value for money into perspective. If the labour cost is one sixth of a western minimum wage, the price should reflect that. The margins on new house builds and on car sales are significantly higher than in the UK or the States, and import taxes on foreign goods often put the price up to a western equivalent or higher.

I went back to work the day after I arrived back in Blighty and was pretty tired by the time I got home in the evening. I envy people who seem to have no problems with jet lag. The atmosphere in the office was cold and unpleasant. Everyone appeared to be watching their backs for the next installment of whatever management game was coming next and the extra workload that that would entail. The completion documents on the house were going to be signed on Tuesday so I arranged to take the afternoon off. "That's very inconvenient," I was told. I was taking it as a half day of my holiday entitlement and surely a few hours to sign legal documents on the sale of one's own house was normal practice and not unreasonable.

All went well at the solicitor's though the ex and I neither spoke to each other nor looked each other in the eye. You could cut the atmosphere with a knife. In Thailand, there would have been smiles all-round, even if they were not genuine smiles of happiness. We did manage to speak to each other a little over the weekend. I had already worked out what I would keep and what I would discard from my possessions in the granny annex where I was living. The ex and I walked around the house to decide what we would each take from the main house and arrange for the rest to be taken to the local recycling centre. It's amazing what you collect but never use and do not really need over some sixteen years of marriage. Old fashioned cd and record players. The spare washing machine in the outhouse that we never used.

Some of my gardening and do it yourself tools could be sold to the buyer of our house or sold through an advert in the local newspaper. We would split the proceeds, she said. I never saw much of that money. She wanted to keep the stamp collection that we had built up together "for sentimental reasons." It was not valuable, just new issue English stamps and stamps we bought from our holidays abroad together or given to us by friends. I used to look at the albums occasionally. She never did. She was totally uninterested. But, if she wanted them, I was not prepared to argue. She could have them.

I hired a truck for the next day and we went to the council yard together. I handled the heavier stuff and she carried the lighter bundles to the various skips. One of the first things to go was her "sentimental" stamp collection.

When I got home I buried my head in my hands and cried. I could not understand why she could be so cruel. I went on the internet and sent an email to Toy. I didn't mention what had happened but it cheered me up to be able to write a few words to her.

Got to the bank on the Monday morning and was called in to the boss's office before I had a chance to take my coat off and sit down. One of my workmates suggested I put some padding in the back of my trousers. "You are being called into the headmaster's study, Derek," he told me. I grinned widely. I was told that the bank was taking a serious view of my taking a few hours off work. I asked if this was a change of policy, that contractual holiday entitlements were no longer being honoured. No answer. The tirade went on. He did all the talking from then on. I was spending more time in Thailand or on the sick list than I spent working in the bank. That I was working to cover the extra workload that had been placed on me, seemed to count for nothing.

The bank was continually downsizing. The technique habitually used was to find fault with one's work until you gave up and left of your own accord. It was standard practice. The strain gets to you in the end. My interview with the big boss went on for a full hour. I had had enough. You can take my one month's notice, I said. There is still some holiday due to me so I will leave in three weeks' time. Until then, I'll do my job but don't put other work on my desk. It won't get done. I'll do what I'm paid to do. I turned and walked out. I never spoke or saw him again. The relief was overwhelming. I felt as if a weight had been lifted off my shoulders. Difficult to explain how happy and stress-free I felt.

I would work out my notice, get my ticket sorted out for Thailand, and in less than one month I would be with Toy. I had nowhere else to go anyway. The completion date was fixed. I would have to get out. I had no leaving party and just got up and left on my last day. A smile, a quick
"cheerio" and I was away. My flight was in two days' time. I had kept Toy informed of my travel arrangements and what was happening with the house. I spared her the more unpleasant details of what had been going on. I don't think she would have comprehended how western people can act in such circumstances. She would not have believed me if I had told her.

I did have a strange sense of leaving everything behind. All I had worked for. The house and garden. Would I miss my friends? Many I had not seen lately. I had spent a lot of time in Thailand and when you are divorced you suddenly don't get invited out to social functions as much. It was only much later that I would realise that some of what we take for granted in England does not exist in Thailand. Thais are not great book lovers and there are few libraries in Thailand. I think they are mainly in Bangkok and the universities.

I missed popping down the pub and having a chat and a joke with the locals. Only when you have left permanently do you appreciate what you had before.

I had booked the taxi to the airport for 10 in the morning and arranged to see Michael to say my goodbye. Just before 9.30, my ex-wife drove out of the drive with my son in the front seat. They had disappeared into the distance by the time I ran outside the annex to try to stop the car.
The taxi was on time. I got in. I never looked back.

Chapter 10 Burning My Boats

It was a strange feeling arriving in Thailand without a return ticket in my pocket. I felt I had escaped and that I could no longer go back. That I had burnt my boats. That I had made a decision I could not now change. Would I see Michael again? Would we be able to keep in touch? I felt like I was starting out on a new adventure and that I was losing my old life. I was relieved about that but I did not want to lose Michael. That part I wanted to keep.

Toy's first words were, "You're in my country now." That gave me a feeling of security and made me less anxious. I was glad to be with Toy again and with someone whom I could trust. She had eased me in to Thai life before. She could do so again. I would not be alone. It was the first time she had ever used the words, "you're in my country now." It was comforting and welcoming. Later, I was to realise that I should have put a different interpretation on what she said. You live and learn.

Thai laws and customs can be frustrating to a foreigner more used to a western view of life. I was pleased to meet my old friends again. Mali, Pakpao, and Wilai always smiled and gave me a *wai* whenever they saw me. I was still a frequent visitor at the school. I knew few other Thais and those I knew were really friends or associates of Toy. It dawned on me only much later that I was not building up my own social group among the Thais. I was sort of integrating but only vicariously through Toy. I was not making my own friends. Take Toy out of the equation and I would become the typical lonely *farang*.

We have most of our meals at restaurants rather than cooking at home. That was okay when I was on holiday but, as a permanent arrangement, it was becoming expensive. More often than not, we ate with friends and I always took care of the tab. In Thailand, it is the older or more senior person who pays. Custom or not, this was an outlay I could not afford on a regular basis. We tried to limit our evening excursions to just a few times a week and to do more home cooking. I have always liked making my own meals, anyway. I was looking forward to experimenting with a few western recipes for Toy to try. She liked the occasional meal, but we still tended to eat out most evenings.

Thai food is inexpensive and I like most dishes so long as they are not too spicy. Some of the roadside stalls offer tasty and properly cooked food but there is not a great deal of variety. For around 40 or 50 baht you can have a typical Thai meal with rice or noodles. Pork or chicken is the most common choice for a meat to put on your rice but you do not get much. Meals are served with a thin soup which is basically hot water flavoured with some Thai vegetables and meat. Cold iced water is freely available. Restaurants had more choice and always had air con and you could order a beer. Of course, more expensive. This was Toy's usual choice for somewhere to eat. I craved for the occasional McDonald's and usually once a week we would eat at a western owned pub or restaurant. At those pubs in the centre of Chiangmai, the Thai meals were a little more expensive than at Thai owned establishments and the western food was certainly dearer. They were always crowded with *farangs* and their wives or girlfriends. With such a captive market, one could see how they could get away with higher prices. Wholesale food costs and labour are cheap in Thailand and these restaurants make better margins than they would if they operated in a western country.

To be honest, it is a bit of a fight to get Toy to realise we can't eat out very night. I am not a "cheap Charlie" as she calls some *farangs*, but I don't have endless resources. We get to see Kanya a lot more than we used to. She's a bright and lively young lady and she's good company. But you can have too much of a good thing and as I have said, I don't have a limitless source of cash from my atm. We'll have to establish some ground rules on how often we meet as a threesome. I hope Toy will be my wife pretty soon and as much as I love Kwang and will do anything for her, I see Toy and myself as a couple who can be alone together most of the time. Thais are so family oriented that they can't seem to switch them off for even one minute. A clash of cultures, I suppose. We'd expect to see family regularly in the West, but not as often as the Thais do.

We still spent time visiting markets and temples. Sometimes they are very similar and you think you've seen it all before. Then you visit one that is so different with a character of its own that you can't resist taking a score of photos. I never get bored at browsing round the street markets with their distinctive smells of cooking and the fresh odours of fruits like Durian. I don't tire of the craft shops. Maybe I will one day but for the moment I find them very interesting. I've always been a great one for window shopping. In Thailand, of course, there aren't any windows! The traders display all their wares in the open, only rushing to cover them when the skies darken and the refreshing rain comes. You tend to get a good downpour and not a drizzle. It commonly lasts only a quarter of an hour or so. Having written that, we'll now probably get a four hour tropical storm and have to batten down all the hatches!

The smiles, the apparent happiness and contentment with life that is so essentially Thai. Unless you have been here it is almost impossible to describe how the whole atmosphere of Thailand gets to you. It's so easy to forget some of the realities of life here. I suppose I'm going through a honeymoon period with the country. Toy tries to explain how we should live for today and not worry about tomorrow. This is the *mai pen rai* attitude that every Thai has. Whatever will be, will be. I can identify with it to some extent. I think it is less stressful and it puts minor frustrations into perspective. I get used to going along to an appointment and finding the office is closed for the day. No warning, no apology. You book a restaurant meal and they're closed when you turn up. It doesn't bother me as much as it used to but I understand why some *farangs* just can't hack it. You have to be Thai and have this "it doesn't matter" view of life. It does not always work for me. I still get uptight from time to time, however much Toy says I shouldn't.

We go to quite a lot of functions including school events. It has always amazed me how many people turn up in Thailand for weddings, funerals, house-warmings, and so on. They are basically social events for all the community to join in, at funerals especially. It's a country where a friend of your friend becomes your friend too. Thais will travel great distances to attend the funeral of someone they last met at school and whom they only occasionally meet or chat on the phone. I'm finding more and more differences between how we do things in the West compared with how it happens here.

We meet many people at these get-togethers. There is always some distant connection with Toy. The last one we went to was for the wedding of the daughter of a friend of Toy's boss. We'd never met her or her family. Everyone had a great time and we gave the usual cash envelope which is traditional in Thailand. A local dignitary gave the main speech. I think he was a former member of parliament. A Thai family will always try to find someone important on occasions like these. He does not have to have any links with the family.

House hunting became a daily event for us and I enjoyed it immensely. There were so many on offer and the sales staff were bending over backwards to show you around. Glasses of water were refreshed as you walked around the *moobaan* (estate) from show house to show house. Young girls came rushing up with umbrellas when the sun got hot. This show of caring kindness is so typical of the Thai. Not only is it endearing but you get addicted to it. You begin to expect it all the time. It's usually genuine but you sometimes wonder if it is just to impress the Westerner who has money. The show houses are meticulous. They are swept several times a day, the garden is carefully manicured, and the furniture on display instinctively makes you want to buy the property.

You won't of course get the furniture if or when you buy. And, as we found out later, you don't get the same quality in the house you actually purchase either. Maybe punters should wait to purchase the show house when the *moobaan* has reached the end of its selling program. We must have visited about twenty such estates developed by different companies until we found the location and size house we wanted and which I could afford.

We looked at some houses that were not in gated communities. I quite liked some but Toy was not at all keen. She said most *farangs* wanted the security that these *moobaans* offered and, as she had said to me before, liked the added benefits of a clubhouse and swimming pool which most provided. I didn't realise, and perhaps she didn't either, that these facilities come with a cost. And you pay whether you use them or not. Your water and electricity charges are higher than the costs levied by the utility companies as the developer will add on his own margin. Once the site is fully sold, security may not be so frequent and garbage collection may not be as regular. Maintenance jobs may not be so promptly attended to. It depends on the developer. Some are better than others. Her other point was that I would be more likely to meet fellow Westerners in a *moobaan* than in an ordinary Thai village. That sounded a persuasive argument and we signed up with a new build some twenty kilometers from Chiangmai. It's a convenient location and not so big that you feel there's not much of a community spirit. There are some foreigners here but I don't meet them often.

Thais can be very persuasive. Without arguing, they get their way by making repeated suggestions. Toy may well be right about farangs always preferring to live in gated moobaans. Never having lived in an ordinary Thai village, I cannot really judge. Only one of my expat friends lives in a village and he seems to like it, probably easier for him to get to know his neighbours and join in village activities. I tend to go along with Toy's ideas. I don't speak Thai and outside our own social circle, I don't know any Thais personally. All the Thais I associate with are really Toy's friends or coworkers. Perhaps I should try to create more space for myself and get out a bit more and have a fresher group of friends, whether Thai or *farang*. I must give it some thought.

Toy works every day and sometimes has to do a "duty" day at weekends. Usually once a month, when she supervises pupils at the boarding school. She either takes the car or I drop her off. As a rule we go out somewhere near her school for lunch. As I am home all day I do my share of the household chores. I don't wear an apron all day long but I'm proficient at loading and unloading washing machines and my ironing skills are second to none.

Facebook, Youtube, and the internet are godsends for the expat. You can download a great deal from the UK BBC sites. It keeps you up to date with the foreign news and you can catch up with your favourite soaps or programmes. I cycle each morning to get my Bangkok Post, the daily Thai newspaper in English for expats. On occasion, I've written into their postbag if a topic interests me. So, I keep myself occupied.

My routine for the next weeks will be different, however. I'm getting married to Toy.

She does not want a formal wedding or party, though we will have some friends round after we sign all the registers at the *amphur*, the local government office. I'll open a bottle of bubbly. It took just twenty minutes at the office. I had prepared all my documentation in advance; passport, visa, permission to stay, a letter from the British consul to certify that I was free to marry. Only a nominal charge from the Thai *amphur*. The consulate's fee was several thousand baht and they made no checks, I just signed an affidavit. I had to go back twice to get the letter. The operation at the Thai government office was much slicker. An efficient production line, but it got the job done.

A great party in the evening. Neither of us really wanted a big fuss, we'd both been married before. Her father lives in Tak, a long way away, so he could not come. We'll pop down there next weekend as we need to pay a nominal dowry, the Thai *sinsot*. But tonight we'll spend the evening with friends and eat and drink the night away to celebrate the start of my married life in Thailand with the Thai goddess I first met those many years ago on an internet site.

Chapter 11 Feeling Alone

Although I feel happily married in Thailand, I still think about how I'm coping with what is in reality a very unusual life style and if I am truly integrating into this country.

I don't think marrying Toy was love on the rebound. I don't believe it was a reaction from a failed western marriage. We had had some fun together and she is a most caring lady. We are blissful enough together and enjoy each other's company, I suppose. We don't see much of each other during the day. I am at my computer; she's teaching in the classroom. Computers can get addictive but I get pleasure watching Youtube and the UK television channels. If I need a break, I'll do a few chores around the house. Some days, I take her to school and we have lunch together. If I am at home and Toy is at work, I fill my time by sitting down watching films on my computer or writing on Facebook. Occasionally, I'll help out teaching English at Toy's school. Nothing serious: reciting English nursery rhymes, pointing to parts of the body and asking them for the name in English, teaching them colours, counting the numbers one to ten, and other light exercises in learning. I enjoy it. They enjoy it. I do get tired quickly which the teachers have noticed and they have expressed concern. Having now taught in a modest sort of way, I now appreciate how tired and stressed teachers can become when standing in front of a class of 30 to 40 pupils all day long.

Our evenings are, more often than not, spent eating and relaxing at a local hostelry. I keep Fridays free for a coffee with a few expat friends though Toy sometimes has made other arrangements for the day and I have to cancel at the last minute. Toy goes upstairs whenever a *farang* comes round to see me. She is rather shy, but she does not do that with her Thai friends.

I spoke with two friends of mine about expats in Thailand and how some fit in here better than others. Over a few coffees, we pieced together some very short pen portraits of those we knew. I have used their words whenever I can. Sometimes they are repeating what I have said in earlier chapters.

Paul is an interesting character. He lives just a few hundred yards away on this housing development. I fell out with him, so we don't speak to each other anymore. I admit I spend some time surfing the Thai internet forums as I did in the UK. He appears to spend the whole of his time glued to a computer screen. He is a bit contrarian, always disagreeing with whatever a poster says. That seems par for the course on almost all Thai forums. New members particularly get a right old bashing in the flame wars. I tend to skip those arguments and read only topics of interest and those that may be useful. I read more than I post. Most expats say they do the same. Take the posts with a pinch of salt, but surf a few forums for yourself and you will get what I mean. The least biased forum for *farangs*, in my view, is http://www.andrew-drummond.com. Now blocked in Thailand. A freelance journalist with experience in the UK press, he is a bit of a terrier when it comes to discussing expat issues. He won't let go when he takes up a reader's case. He has exposed many foreigners in Thailand who have cheated their fellow expats.

Matt and I agreed that, although there are some posters that can see both sides of an issue, most seem to be either Thai bashers or Thai apologists. Taking extreme views as if everything was only ever black or white in this country. I think some of the bashers have been badly burned here and have lost a great deal of money. The bulk of their life savings may have disappeared through property scams or putting everything in the name of a Thai wife or girlfriend. Thai law does not allow land ownership by a foreigner. These posters argue about dual pricing and what they consider a bias against the *farang* when it comes to resolving disputes. They have a point but they never seem to see the Thai side of an argument or that there are other more pleasant aspects of life in Thailand.

Paul is a basher if ever there was one. In small doses he can be interesting to talk to but many of his stories seem a bit far-fetched. To be fair, he was more reasonable in face to face conversations. Forums where you post anonymously can make some posters more aggressive.

Toy disappeared whenever he came round to see me.

Then there's **Alfie**, whom I know only through an internet forum. A complete contrast. He's a model Thai Apologist. His standard response to a news report on the murder rate or road fatality rate in Thailand is to say that you get violent deaths in all countries in the world. Of course, he's right. The issue, though, is how much more often it happens here compared with elsewhere. He won't accept that. To him everything in the garden smells sweet when he wears his rose-tinted glasses.

I hope I'm more objective and not so biased. Though I suppose I do like to put the more unpleasant aspects of life here to the back of my mind. It's a *mai pen rai* response, I think. If you can do nothing about it, no point thinking about it. Let it go. Don't stress yourself. It will not change anything. It's also a common Thai response and Thai apologists follow suit. In the West we accept criticism about our countries. We actively join in the fray; Thais think it's wrong to criticise their homeland.

Thais have to be happy with their lot. Revolutionary ideas do not come naturally to the Thai. Nevertheless, when they are pushed too far they do let rip and demonstrations can get out of hand. During the October 1973 riots at Thammasat University, the King called for calm and peace but was even handed in his condemnation of both sides. The various coups by the military, the actions of big business, and the élite; all show there was an appetite for change. But demonstrating for such causes is certainly not a trait Thais are comfortable with. They prefer avoiding conflict. Keeping the status quo would have avoided a lot of bloodshed.

As Matt said, Thais can be suspicious of their partners getting too close or familiar with other expats. They don't know what advice and comments their partners may be receiving which could change their own relationship with "their" *farang*. There was a ring of truth in what he said. I do get embarrassed when Toy suggests a change of plan when I have arranged to meet some expats or when she disappears when they come round to see me. I don't show my feelings and I make excuses, but they feel snubbed, I am sure.

Thai wives do come across as being possessive of their partners, especially if they are *farang*. It is as if they are saying, "keep away, he's mine." Westerners are said to be *poo dee angkrit* as they are perceived to be more malleable than Thai men. *Poo*, a word that does not sound too good to a western listener though it is actually a term of great respect in Thai, is used for example for judges and senior government ministers. *Dee* is good, *angkrit* is English. Ask a Thai what they find characteristic of a person they call *poo dee angkrit* and they will tell you it means someone (not necessarily English. It could be any Westerner) who is generous, caring, trusting, polite. These are the adjectives they will commonly use. A Thai can wrongly assume that these characteristics indicate naivety and may try to take advantage.

Most Thais are aware that some foreigners, particularly those who are fluent in Thai, are quite astute and are *au fait* with how Thais do things. They can understand what the Thai is saying and comprehend some of the aspects of Thainess that Thais would prefer them not to contemplate. I remember an example that Paul often quoted about his friend, Janet.

Janet was in a car with her friend when it hit a motorcyclist who had come out of a *soi* without paying attention. It had crossed the lane in which she was driving to get to the other side of the road. Janet's friend swerved to avoid him but clipped the rear end of his bike. It was plainly the biker's fault. He did not have right of way. His bike was straddled across the carriageway. Janet's friend had not been speeding and had done all she could to avoid the collision. But, he was Thai. The police came quickly and drew chalk marks round the positions of the car and bike. They took statements. The biker had little money with him but his bike was badly damaged. The car had only minor scratches and some chips in the paintwork. Janet heard the policeman tell the biker that the *farang* would be held responsible.

"You pay," were the only words the officer spoke when he went over to Janet's expat friend. Having to pay when not at fault is not only for *farang*. Well-off Thais have to do the same, they would usually volunteer a payment. Not to do so would mean losing face.

I had an internet problem and the technician wanted 3000 baht to replace some wiring. I did what a Thai would do, I asked to see the wire he took out. He could not show me. He had not replaced the wire at all. I intended not paying the full amount; Toy said we would have to pay it otherwise we would lose face and appear mean and stingy. He would lose face for having been caught out. Paying would be better for both parties, she said, however rationally we argued. The solution would be not to use him again. This face concept just would not occur in the West and, although I accept it as a cultural quirk, I admit I do not fully follow the logic.

If a taxi driver or motor bike taxi took you to the wrong place, you need to pay. He may have misunderstood you but he has spent time and fuel getting you there. That is the Thai logic for both Thai and foreign customers.

With the motor cyclist, it then became a question of how much to settle for. Janet, listening to the conversation, knew that the rider was suggesting twice the normal rate because the accident involved a *farang*. She negotiated the price downwards. It makes the point that Thais do not like those *farangs* who, usually because they speak the language, know what's going on, and cannot be easily fobbed off. They refer to them as *kon roo reuang (*literally, someone who knows the story.) We would probably say of such a person, "there are no flies on him," someone who knows too much about what is going on.

One of my friends recalled **Nolan,** a Swiss guy who always dressed in Lanna costume, telling him that the Thais don't think like us. It was an obvious comment, rather a throwaway line. Neither he nor I thought anything of it at the time. On reflection, I think he's right. Nothing is in reality that serious to the Thai mind. *Mai pen rai* overrides most of their actions. It doesn't matter. Westerners get serious over even minor issues.

Apart from some western occupied houses, homes are not earthed. Electricity is different in Thailand! That comment came from a Thai electrician and he genuinely believed it. Justifying an action as being right is an attribute that you will notice frequently in your relationships with a Thai. Perhaps they are impervious to doubt; perhaps they like making up a story and embellishing the facts just to rationalise what they do.

Asking, "Do you think doing it this way is better?" would be the Thai way to get around their not doing an electrical job the way you want it done. Most definitely, do not raise your voice or get angry. Thai managers have a slight lead over the *farang* manager. As they are Thai, they are automatically given respect by their workers. They have higher status and the worker cannot easily question an instruction. The *farang* does not have that benefit. It is harder for him. The best way forward is to speak calmly and politely, not rush in by arguing, and be as persuasive and complimentary as you can.

Thais have a stronger belief in Karma, the law of cause and effect, than we do. Your harmful thoughts, ideas, and actions will return to haunt you. As you sow, so shall you reap. Retribution for what you do will get back to you. Yes, Nolan had given many examples showing they don't think like us. We need to get on their wavelength without completely throwing away our own western standards and way of thinking.

Louis has found that balance. He was looking for someone who would care for him as he got older and with whom he could share his life. His wife's goal was to find a *farang*. It is a key reason why Thai women choose foreigners. As I said before, Toy had had a bad experience with a Thai man. The reason she had been on an English language internet site in the first place was to chat and date with a *farang*. Louis is Belgian; Gop, his Thai wife, is a retired teacher. They have an understanding in their relationship. They live happily together and are under no illusions why their marriage is working out so well. She cares for him. He provides her with the security that all Thais need. He is older and he knows she will continue to look after him when he gets less mobile or ill. Thais are very family oriented. They look after their elders. Old folks' homes are abhorrent to them. Caring comes naturally to a Thai, it is built into their thinking.

They met in Belgium and he accepted that her purpose in marrying him was to ensure her own future and not to find the most handsome man on earth. My friends know several expats who honestly believe they were chosen as a marriage partner for their looks and charisma. They should re-think and consider the reality. *To thine own self be true.*

Every time we see Louis and Gop, they appear in high spirits and contented. They both know the score. They both understand why they married and the benefits they both get from the relationship.

I introduced **Daniel** and **Emily** to some of the teachers in Toy's school and they became interested in helping out in the infant English classes. The school organised some positions for them in other schools with whom they have contact. They visit Thailand every year for an extended holiday, staying in guesthouses. They like to get involved with the locals and doing some teaching in between visits to various attractions fits in well with their holiday plans. I think teaching at that level can be very beneficial for the pupils. Technically work permits are required, but blind eyes are turned as they are providing a useful service.

Chapter 12   A Reality Check

Although Toy stayed in school for lunch today, I did not feel hungry so poured myself a few drinks to while away the afternoon. I habitually have a liquid lunch nowadays. Two friends came round and we sat down to have a few beers and talk about some of the expats they know and how they are handling life in Thailand. Nolan and Daniel get about much more than I do, they meet more people, and I learn much about Thailand from their observations.

First, there's **Alex**. They said he is a nice chap. An American gay who lives in a rented house with his young Thai partner. He inherited some money from his mum when she died and splashes it around a bit. Sometimes he is a little opinionated, particularly when he wants Thais to behave more like Americans. His pet beef is the slow service he gets in restaurants and Thais never turning up on time for appointments.

His friends remind him that Thailand is not the 51st state of America. It makes no impression. He will never fully adapt to or appreciate Thai life. Nevertheless, he is happy enough living the way he wants to live. I do not think he wants to integrate and sees no benefit in doing so. No problem with that, it's up to him. As with most Americans, he can be extremely generous and enjoyable company.

Gabriel, who is French, is a manager for a French company operating in Thailand. He has been here several years now and he will argue with a Thai and will call a spade a spade. He says turning the other cheek and walking away does not solve problems. Whether they lose face or not, the job needs to be done properly the way he wants it. As the boss, he can get away with it but it is not a Thai way of doing things. They prefer a more subtle and easy-going approach from managers. Maybe he needs to get them on side. Maintaining good relationships with the workforce is vital in any business.

My friends thought that he should strive for a better balance by accepting some cultural norms but not letting them ride roughshod over his own way of getting projects completed on time. A bit of cultural give and take. Not easy.

Sophie is English. She lived with her toy boy for several years but they live separate lives now. She rarely sees him. She certainly spent money on him and they did a lot of things together. He was never interested in meeting her *farang* friends. Initially, she claimed it was Thai shyness though I think she later understood that he wanted her financial support but not to share her life.

Sophie speaks reasonable Thai and integrates into the local community, helping out at the local dog rescue. Like all foreigners, she gets frustrated at times but she quickly catches herself if she is responding in a non-Thai way. She speaks calmly – Thais don't like argument or loud voices. She has more *mai pen rai* in her than most *farangs.* She understands you do not get too forceful or serious with a Thai. Speaking a little of the language, not raising her voice, accepting a few inconveniences, not having too great an expectation from whatever a Thai does, and an understanding of concepts such as face, *mai pen rai*, *greng jai*, have helped her to fit in.

She can be a little over generous in paying Thais for work done. Some will take advantage of her bighearted nature. She was caught once by overspending on her toy boy. As her bank balance declines – she is in her fifties, retired early, and has no job – Sophie is getting more careful.

Lucas had been sold a house on a development by a group of Dutch nationals but he did not get the specification that he had paid for and the property was nothing like the photos he had seen at the sales promotion. Daniel said Lucas had been led to believe that he owned the house but in fact it was registered, as it has to be under Thai law, in the name of a Thai. The term "nominee" is a misnomer and it is illegal for foreigners to own land under a nominee. The property is owned outright by the Thai. Any money given by the foreigner has to be by way of a gift and is recorded as such.

He continued living in the house with his Thai girlfriend but would not pay the final balance due under the contract. Court procedures would have dragged on for years and there were irregularities in the paperwork. The Dutch group did not pursue it but then neither did he get any money back from a house he paid for but did not own. That stays with the Thai "nominee."

Lucas had met his girlfriend in a bar and rented a shop at a modest rental so that she could sell furniture from it. Long term it may have made a reasonable profit but the family moved in as "helpers" so there was no cash left at the end of each day. A Dutch couple lived a few doors away from his house, and they tried to warn him about Dokmai, his girlfriend. Sometimes a same-nationality couple living together can see a situation more clearly than a man with a Thai partner. But it is never wise to get between a man and his girl, however tactful and well-intentioned you are.

He would not accept what was actually going on.

He had many friends here. Everyone liked Lucas. He was good company. A pity it did not work out for him. He cut his losses and is now back in the Netherlands.

George married a Thai and they lived in England for six years. Suda is a nice lady apparently. George gets frustrated very quickly with Thai ways. Dual pricing, corruption, bad workmanship, Thai drivers, appointments never being kept, Thais not saying what they really mean. His wife tries to explain that Thais do not do things in a western way. She has lived abroad so can perhaps understand his frustrations.

Unfortunately, Thais don't seem keen to follow through with the advice foreigners need to adapt to life here. They see it as arguing with their partners, when in fact it could be of immense help to them. Toy is the same. I wish she would put in plain words how I should react to certain situations. Thai culture is new to me and to many expats. They need some help in getting over culture shock and learning how to integrate, or at least live in harmony here.

Nolan, one of the friends who had come round, had read the book "Thailand Fever" last week and he is going to give George and Suda a copy. Written by an American and his Thai wife, it is primarily about Thai - western relationships but it is a store of useful advice on how Thais and Westerners can get along together. The book is in both English and Thai so encourages a couple to read it together. It seems a great way for them to look at what they both see as a few of the petty irritations of living in Thailand. Thailand Fever illustrates how they can deal with them better. I wanted Toy to read it with me some time ago but she is too busy at school. A pity, the book is an effective antidote to culture shock.

Bill, who is in his late seventies, does not speak Thai and has no Thai friends. He enjoys a good chinwag with expats but is not too keen on expat clubs. He is a bit of a loner. Bill enjoys English documentaries on the TV and keeps up with the news. When he is discussing something, he is usually right. He is quite knowledgeable and has worked at several jobs in many countries. He does not need to show off and is no bull-shitter.

Some expats here do tend to pretend to be what they are not. In their home country, you would ignore them. Here, because there are fewer Westerners, it is harder to escape them. Expats gravitate towards other expats and befriend one other. It is a natural reaction. You would not do that so automatically in the West. You would pick and choose your acquaintances.

Bill's only foible is that he can be a little jealous of others. That can happen in Thailand if you have been caught in a scam or lost money and then meet someone who has been more fortunate than you. It can be difficult to accept that they have the level of wealth that you formerly had.

Tim, Nit's husband, is Dutch. They bought a new house here and he ran (with a permit) his business from there. The company he worked for then promoted him and he moved back to the Netherlands with Nit. She loves it there, despite the weather. They now have a young daughter who will be tri-lingual; English, Thai, Dutch. Nit had made it clear in her university days that she wanted to marry a *farang*. Not all her friends are envious. Not all congratulate her on her good fortune.

Samuel is a retired consultant from the UK and he has a portfolio of apartments both there and in Thailand. For some reason, he cannot keep any friend for very long. He is a born know-it-all. His bragging can get a bit repetitive. His sole conversation is about the money he is making from his condominiums and how he is spending it. One of my friends said that he gives monthly updates on how much he spends on air conditioning. Good luck to him and I am sure he works very hard. It cannot be easy having to keep an eye on a string of properties and tenants.

Quite a few expats have a tendency to boast and talk big. It does not apply to Sam but it always amazes me how many PhDs, ex-SAS and ex American Naval Seals we have as retirees in Thailand! If it were true, we would need several large aircraft if they all had to return to their native countries at the same time. I have never met one but they habitually take over on some of the internet forums that I read.

Nolan knows two families who immigrated to France and said that, as in his native
Switzerland, expats in France do not know why a few expats who live here tend to brag. Neither Nolan nor Daniel could offer an explanation why that happens in Thailand.

Sam met his wife in Bangkok. He says she came from a poor family and lived in a slum. No-one knows the circumstances of how they got to know each other. Boong speaks extremely good English and is the only Thai that my friends know who reads English books. Samuel and Boong have a five-year-old girl who, of course, has dual nationality and can speak English and Thai. Boong reads books on childcare, she is that fluent. Sam says they met as they both had similar interests. Nobody knows much about her background.

Leon and **Julie** are Swiss. They have had a house built to their own design and to a very high specification. Heaven knows how much it cost. Julie was a language teacher so probably did not find learning Thai that difficult. She deals with all the building queries. They have a mix of Thai and *farang* friends. A healthy combination,

I think. Leon is a retired barrister and what he found strange when they first came to Thailand was how impossible it is to get Thais to tell you something in a straightforward manner, to tell you what's on their mind. As a lawyer, Leon is used to thinking analytically and weighing up what people say. He used a questioning approach to bring out the truth in court.

It can be frustrating when you learn that such a method does not work in Thailand. People are more layback, do not like conflict situations, and are reticent in giving out information. Partly, because they do not want to offend or lose face. They make up stories, rather than consider how to present the facts, for that very reason.

Andrew and **Elisabeth** have just moved house. They are an English couple who had bought their property five years ago (in the name of a Thai) but decided they would prefer to rent in future. By selling, they released capital. A prudent move as they could never have left it to their children. It was Thai owned. They wanted more land anyway as their garden was rather small. They had no problem selling the house. Their Thai "owner" willingly signed the transfer papers.
They lost about 20% on the deal as, unlike in the West, houses depreciate. Finding a *farang* buyer will get you a higher figure, particularly if the house is to western standards.

Both Daniel and Nolan said that Thais value land more than houses and prefer to knock down a house and build again to their own better design. If someone has died in the house, they will almost certainly re-build. Thais go for spacious interiors so that visiting relatives can camp out on the floors. It is quite normal to provide a blanket or a mattress on the floor for guests. If you go inside a Thai home, you will see minimal furniture.

Ruby is a single lady in her seventies who lives with a guy she calls her toy boy. Namsom is thirty years her junior. Ruby does not want to get married nor own a property in Thailand. She has paid his tuition fees for music classes and has set him up in a small business venture. They argue about marrying and buying a property occasionally but Ruby is quite adamant in what she wants to do.

Namsom is enjoying a better lifestyle than if he was with a Thai. Ruby has his company and is looked after. It is a win-win arrangement.

Edward has been sensibly cautious. He was dating a Thai teacher in Bangkok for just under a year. They were getting on well together, but increasingly there were demands for new clothes, furniture, and a new car was hinted at. He packed his bags.

After a little while, he found a very down to earth Isaan lady that shared his interests in life and, like him, enjoyed the outdoor country life. Mamuang (her Thai nickname, meaning Mango), has two teenage children who live with them. Edward waited two years before popping the question. They seem to have a good life together. His friends like her. That is always a good sign. A lesson perhaps: never rush in, think carefully on what could be warning signs, and appreciate that people from the East give out different body signals from Westerners. Understanding the culture is key.

Edward had not been blind to the downsides of Thailand. Like most expats here, he could see the good and the bad. On balance, he likes it here and plans to stay. He does not fully understand all the ramifications of the cultural differences that he observes every day. That could be exasperating if it were not for Mamuang's help and explanations. Without some Thai input, some expats find they have an uneasy feeling in living here.

Richard is fascinated by the Thai life style and is one of those *farangs* that observes carefully how Thais live their lives. He takes one long holiday every year with his English girlfriend, backpacking their way around Asia. Thailand remains his favourite destination. Jennifer is a little naive and does not always take in the subtler nuances that Richard understands. He is on the same wavelength as the Thai, despite not being a permanent resident.

Daniel, pouring himself another drink, spoke of an English couple who teach in Thailand and who similarly understand Thai ways. The lady, whose name he had forgotten, told him of an incident where she had parked her car when she was doing some voluntary teaching in a government institution. She returned to find someone accusing her of having damaged another parked vehicle. There was no point arguing, she paid up. She had understood that it was a way of getting a richer *farang* to finance a repair. If the authorities had been made aware of the episode, they may have stepped in, but she did not think it was worth causing a fuss. Interestingly, a similar true story is narrated in *Thailand Take Two*.

The Thai bashers and the Thai apologists hold forth on internet forums and in the bars. The majority of expats are, however, more balanced in their views and observations of Thai life.
The honorary consuls need to be discrete and diplomatic but they are aware that there are two sides to Thailand. Very wise words from eighty-year-old **Owen**, who spent thirty years of his life here. "There are things I don't like about Thailand, but there are things I don't like about England too. Go with the flow."

Chapter 13   Expat Clubs

I found on my first visits to Thailand that expat clubs were not for me. Everyone I met was either around my age or older. It was interesting to hear so many English and American accents. Talking to Australians, Dutch, and other nationalities did broaden my outlook on life but it was in a rather anti-Thai, colonial type atmosphere and I knew I would not fit in to that. A few expats were unashamedly canvassing for business. Selling or renting a condo, making a pitch for some investment or insurance business, promoting a massage training school. In a way they were taking advantage of a captive audience who could or would not meet with ordinary Thais to get whatever they wanted. Those present probably did not realise they could get less biased advice and a better deal if they shopped around.

Club members came across as wanting to make money out of the *farang* and with no interest in making Thailand their home or assimilating themselves into the Thai way. They had a habit of repeating themselves often. I imagine we all say the same thing over and over again sometimes. One of the "joys" of getting older. I'm sure I'm guilty of it when I talk of Toy and Thailand.

The betting was that many of these club members y would be back in their home countries in a few years' time. Unquestionably true of some of the committee members. One guy, **Oliver**, actually boasted he did not like Thai food and would never speak a word of Thai. They should learn English, he said. My friends had not met anyone quite like that since but it is disturbing that such people want to stay here, even if they intend returning to their home country later.

It's up to them if they treat Thailand as a long term holiday destination without appreciating the richness of getting to know and integrate with the Thai people. They are missing so much. It's their business though. There's room for all sorts.

Mark, Gilbert, and **Isabel** are regulars in the expat clubs. They don't mix with the locals. Mark helps his wife in her massage school. Gilbert and Isabel host a small discussion group on The Meaning of Life. Apart from the Thai wife of an expat, all the participants are *farang*. Interesting and fruitful as the meetings are, they could just as easily be held on Mars as in Thailand. Gilbert and Isabel are no longer permanent residents, now spending six months in Canada and six months in Thailand each year.

There is a book-reading club run on similar lines. No Thais are present. A gardening club takes a different approach. Thais are encouraged to join in. That appears to be a sensible decision as it taps into a useful source of knowledge. Tropical gardening is not at all like that of the West. It's more fun too when Thais and *farangs*, sharing similar interests, can get together.

Daniel, always the people observer, had to go to the Immigration office to extend his permission to stay. He had got chatting to two expats. One had been in Thailand for over thirty years but, according to Dan, gave the impression that he fell for much of the political propaganda in the English language dailies that are published in Thailand. Talking politics can lead to arguments, so Dan quickly moved on but was amazed that this guy, having been here so long, had no sense of the realities that ordinary Thais could have discussed with him.

The second man had been splitting his time between Thailand and Scotland over the last six years. He had married a dental technician from Bangkok two years ago and had now decided to apply for a retirement visa so that he could move here permanently. He appeared more tuned in to Thai life.

Rachel, a friend of Daniel's, is a retired IT specialist and she is touring the world. It is her first visit to Thailand and she was lodging with an American. They had bitter arguments and she found an alternative place to stay after a few weeks. It was more than a clash of personalities. Rachel could not make him out. His attitude to relationships and his tendency to Thai bash did not blend in with her own ideas on spending time in a foreign country.

Barry has had several live-in girlfriends and eventually married a Malaysian living in Thailand. One year on, he had divorced her by saying "I divorce you" three times. That is probably not valid in Thai law but, anyway, he is now back with her, having had a few platonic relationships in the meantime.

Rachel had chosen to stay where she could meet the ordinary people. That had not worked out when she had rented a room at Barry's but she could not afford to travel the world in luxury and stay in five star hotels. She did not associate with the high society ex-pat crowd. She did not have their money or taste for socialising with other expats and being seen in the coolest nightspots. Everyone to their own taste, of course. But it was not for her. Rachel didn't really know, but she thought that many of them were out of their depth and pretending to be high flyers when they were not. "Living above their class," was how she put it. She felt happier and more relaxed talking to the average Thai and getting to know how they lived.

Robin was a former journalist who had worked with a press agency in Europe. A frequent traveller to Thailand, he had met and married a Thai national and they eventually settled in Bangkok. The marriage grew a bit stale after a while but they still live together. She spends time helping at the local *wat*, he is a keen cyclist and enjoys building items of small furniture for the home. They do most things separately.

He probably thinks that he has no options left other than to make the best of his present situation. It is a dilemma when the main asset, your home, is in the wife's name. They mainly go out for meals, usually with her friends. Sometimes the conversations can be a tad awkward and cold. He has always been a keen reader of Thai history but accepts that there are some subjects that he cannot talk to his wife about.

Robin frequently attended some of the seminars given by Thai universities and which are open to the public. Libraries are not as common in Thailand as in the West and listening to debates was a useful way to keep up with matters of interest. He was a lively contributor in discussion.

Robin had not found it easy to meet people that shared his love for intelligent conversation. It was what he missed most when he retired as a journalist and first arrived in Thailand. Joining these discussion groups allowed him to meet and associate with the kind of people he had previously worked and socialised with and he enjoyed that.

His first impressions of expats in this country were that many were sexpats, would-be high society people, or angry old men who were always finding fault with their adopted country. They may have been in the minority but they made themselves prominent wherever they went. Robin felt he had been lucky to find eventually a group of like-minded foreigners. Not all were white *farangs*, many were Chinese, Singaporean, or from Arab countries.

Outside campus, there were a few clubs which held monthly meetings on topics of interest, not all Thailand or Thai oriented. They tended to be less open and friendly than those in the universities. Cliques were inclined to form and you had the occasional "know-it-all" trying to hold forth. Often an expat who had been here a long time but had had little contact with ordinary Thais.

Robin had got to know **Peter** quite well. Peter was a qualified teacher with a work permit. He worked at a local school teaching English to 15 and 16 year olds and occasionally gave lectures at the university, which is where Robin had met him. His contract will hopefully be renewed each year. School authorities are apt to give out contracts only on a semester or annual basis in Thailand. They are often not renewed. Resources are not always available. Richard has been in post for three years, so clearly they appreciate his skills and dedication. He is not impressed with Thai standards of education but believes they are set to improve as Thailand gets drawn closer into Asean. Better training for teachers to give them fluency in English, less reliance on rote learning in the classroom, and more careful teacher selection would be his three main priorities if he could influence education in Thailand.

Conclusion

Escape to Thailand is not an untypical account of how some expats first get acquainted with the country and then decide to settle here. Many arrive for different reasons and may have similar or dissimilar experiences. Many come for a short holiday and get captivated by the lifestyle and people of a different culture and worldview. The weather is often an attraction for retirees as is the relatively low cost of living. The extremes of heat and rain are not always well considered. Low living costs sometimes come with low quality products and services. Thailand's reputation as a sex hotspot is a magnet for some.

The early chapters give each reader an opportunity to be a "fly on the wall" in Derek's love affair with Toy and Thailand. It is by no means judgmental. Readers are asked to consider the doubts that were undoubtedly in his mind and how they would themselves have reacted if they were in his place. They may have questioned some of the comments and descriptions that he made.

Do you think he was in truth settled in Thailand? Or had he little option but to accept that he had burned his bridges and would lose face if he ever returned? His life style is very different from what he had in England. He spends a great deal of time on the internet and at home alone. He likes making visits to schools to teach English and he certainly seems to enjoy doing so. The kids, I am sure, love him to bits.

He talks of cultural differences but is not always convincing. He gets to know about Thai life styles from what he reads or from what he is told and not always from personal experience or observation. Is he being too naive and trusting? Could there be problems around the corner? He owns no house or land. He speaks no Thai. Apart from some expat friends, he knows only Toy's friends and those he meets at school. How will he feel in his eighties and nineties when he probably won't have so much social contact and still have no knowledge of the language or any better appreciation of the culture and how normal Thais live?

The last three chapters give short pen portraits of other foreigners who live here. Each one totally dissimilar from the others. If you visit Thailand and meet up with some of your fellow countrymen and women you may recognise the characteristics that those chapters describe.

It is too easy to categorise all expats as either Thai Bashers or Thai Apologists. That is an over simplification. Most expats fit into neither group. Because minorities come across as vociferous advocates of these two extreme positions, visitors can get the wrong impression about the average expat.

Any immigrant not making an attempt to learn even some of the language is going to find it difficult to fit in. That is true of any foreign country. In the Far East, where the culture is so different, the life styles are poles apart from what we are used to in the West. Adjustment to a new country is then not so easy to accomplish. Language and culture should not be barriers to integration. The onus is always on the expat to make the first move. Thais will help in any transition to blending into their society but only if they sense you are making serous attempts to integrate. Adopt a sort of "colonial" attitude of superiority or ignore basic cultural norms and the expat or tourist will – despite the smiles and happy faces – find he is not totally accepted.

In their hearts and minds, Thais are patriotic to the point of xenophobia. Unless you meet them half way and relax into their cultural lifestyle, you will not be liked. Your money will be appreciated, of course. Military and economic aid from foreign countries is never turned away. That does not imply acceptance. It is rather like going to a top London restaurant and lording it over the waiters. They'll smile, be attentive to your every whim, and be polite to your face. In the back kitchen, they'll be cursing and swearing at you with disdain. You pay the bill, give a good tip, but probably leave the restaurant unaware of how they truly feel about you.

Whether you are at the Ritz Restaurant in Piccadilly or whether you are living or visiting Thailand, it is, as the Thais would say, "same, same." Thailand is an extremely status conscious kingdom. It has strict rules of hierarchy among its own people. That is extended to all *farangs* who are here. The ever observant Thai can detect an expat's true position in society more quickly and accurately than perhaps we can. They may smile and agree with you. That does not necessarily mean they believe you are of the status you are trying to portray.

To thine own self be true. If you sincerely try to "fit in" – you don't have to go completely native – you will enjoy and benefit from your time here living in a Thai way in a Thai community.

About the Author

Matt Owens Rees is a seasoned travel writer and anthropologist who now lives in Thailand. *Escape to Thailand* is an account of an expat's move to Thailand and his early days in the country. It is a true real life story. Only names have been changed.

It looks at Thai lifestyles in a different way from the author's other main works on Thai culture that concentrate on how diverse Thai and western cultures can be. The result, however, is the same. It aims to explain cultural and lifestyle differences in a readable way.

Thailand Take Two, A Thailand Diary, The Thai Way of Meekness, and even the novel *The Death of a Thai Godfather*, can in many ways complement a reading of *Escape to Thailand* as they all paint a rich picture of today's Thailand. The "anthropology" is accurate but clearer than some more serious texts available on Thai lifestyle and culture. Matt Owens Rees encourages animated discussion in the lecture theatre as well as at other presentations throughout the country. And the result of these exchanges is a very rich picture of the real Thailand.

Carol Hollinger's book "*Mai Pen Rai Means Never Mind*" became a classic introduction to Thai culture. Matt Owens Rees believes she was right to talk of the *mai pen rai* laid-back attitude as an integral part of a Thai's thinking and way of living. But he was motivated to go further by showing; from observations, research, and particularly conversations with Thais, that there are many other factors that explain why Thais are so unlike Westerners. The Asian concept of face, the Buddhist doctrine of no conflict, the strong family and community values that bind Thais together, and the very strict hierarchical structure of society. All have a strong influence on the Thais and how they live their lives.

You can follow Matt Owens Rees at www.BestThailandBooks.com, his twitter
address is @MattOwensRees, you can email him at
brigydon1@outlook.com, and his Facebook page in Chiangmai,

Thailand is Matt Owens Rees. You are welcome to join the Facebook group page "Discussing the Real Thailand" if you wish to read or comment on anything Thai related. All genuine member requests will be approved.

Extracts from Other Books by Matt Owens Rees

Without spoiling the developing plot, here are some extracts from
The Death of a Thai Godfather.

"It sounded like a shrill whistle. Something flew past Anilek's right
ear. A moment later, another high-pitched sound. He felt something
pierce his neck. The crowd screamed as two motor cyclists raced
away on their powerful machines, throwing their guns away as they
disappeared into the distance.

This was a hit. Anilek collapsed. Was he dead?"

"When he took his wife away from labouring in the fields he was
going contrary to the traditions of generations of his family. They
had felt it a duty to toil for others. It was not their position in society
to have wealth and privilege. Granddad believed that was not an
unalterable status. He did not want to take away what the elite had
but he did want the opportunity to create a business for himself that
would give his family a good livelihood and some security for the
future."

"(Tawin) feels strongly that people get the wrong impression of Thai
"mafia" families. We are no different from other businesses that
work hard and grow in order to secure a family's future. As I said,
we are not all violent gangsters."

"He is right to dislike the murdering side of the Sicilian type mafias
of old. They were vengeful bloodthirsty types who wanted more and
more wealth, more and more power. Family honour for them could
never be compromised. Insults meant public retribution by the most
horrific methods possible. While their attention to business was
paramount, the importance of maintaining family power, prestige,
and face was uppermost in their minds. Our family, by contrast,

makes its decisions solely on business criteria. Our decisions are based on what is best for the life that we have chosen to lead."

"We run our businesses in a fair way, Lek. We have to make tough decisions when people betray us but we are not corrupt in our activities. Greed is the big problem. And, irrespective of what many may say, it is not unique to Thailand and is nothing to do with mafias. Those we trade with do not have complaints about how we interact with them. Those we employ earn good wages and have job security. Our companies are operated with ethical and honest principles."

"That is entirely reasonable and a common sense way of working in my view, said Tawin. It is tragic that mafias have this reputation for rigid, secret, and destructive chains of command. The fact is that our system functions efficiently if done with honesty and respect.

There is no business reason for taking revenge on innocent women and children. That is not the true mafia philosophy. That is not my philosophy."

And from A Thailand Diary 1 January – 31 December

17 November

There's a full moon tonight and there will be crowds of young foreigners at the famous Full Moon Party on the beaches of the island of *Gaw Pangang (sometimes written as Kaw Pangang)* at the southern tip of Thailand. There's never fewer than 10,000 revelers at these events. Around 30,000 around New Year's Eve.

Beer and Thai whiskey are sold in buckets and it's not difficult to buy drugs. A few decades ago, the island was a notorious hippy compound for foreigners with its easy fun-loving lifestyle. Tents would be set up on the shoreline and everyone would sit around the camp fires. Although it's more commercialised these days and the atmosphere has changed somewhat, it stills pulls in the young foreign tourists as if it's a rite of passage for all backpackers on a visit to Thailand.

The beach bars compete to attract their customers with the loudest music from the biggest loudspeakers. Stages are set up for fire-dancing while the less adventurous gyrate their bodies further along the beach or skinny dip in the sea. No one minds the nakedness.

There are no lifeguards and a few tourists have drowned in the past. Rapes and muggings are sometimes reported. Last year there was a murder following a drunken brawl. Ferries take those suffering from being high on drugs or having collapsed through excessive drinking to a local hospital on the mainland.

As everywhere in Thailand, there is some corruption where "fines" are demanded by officials for supposed misdemeanours.

After the ferry leaves for the mainland the next day, the huge operation of cleaning up the broken glass, plastic bottles, condoms, and other discarded debris begins. All to prepare for next month's Full Moon party.

http://www.youtube.com/watch?v=9RsvoN1PV_w

30 September

The pace of life is much faster in Bangkok than up-country.

Jumping on a bus smartly because you know it will move off as soon as you have one foot inside, hanging on tightly at corners, bracing oneself for abrupt stops at traffic lights.

The driver and ticket seller on Thai buses are on commission. The more fares they collect; the higher their earnings. Moving off quickly after picking up a passenger is of the essence. The driver may not even pull in to pick up a sole person waiting at a stop if he knows he can pick up several people at the next one. He has every incentive to get there before a rival bus does.
It can be annoying when he decides to take a short cut, missing out some bus stops. It does not happen often but it does occur. You just get off at the most convenient stop near your original destination or catch another bus going in that direction. Passengers don't object. They take it in their stride, *mai pen rai*. It's no big deal.

Most buses are not air-conditioned, so the windows are open unless there is heavy rain. Fans also help keep the passengers cool.

Tuk tuks can carry two or three passengers, and are more expensive than the buses. You negotiate the fare. The standard practice is to start by halving the amount he suggests and accepting when it's about one third less than his first price. They take you directly to where you want to go. Well, not always. Sometimes he may think it would be better to take you to his brother-in-law's gem shop for some tourist bargains. Smile, say *mai ao* (no thanks, I don't want to go in) and he'll proceed with the journey. He'll accept that. Just don't get annoyed.

Taxis are metered and it is usually best to insist that the drivers use them. Pick another cab if they refuse. Unless you know the area, you may find some drivers will take you on a scenic tour to boost the meter total. But most drivers do not do that. Some are from up-country, so genuinely may not know their way around Bangkok.

Taxis at hotels and airports may add a charge for picking you up there. The drivers often have to pay a fee for queuing in the taxi rank. There is little you can do at an airport. But at hotels, you could easily walk a few metres down the street and hail a cab. The majority of taxi drivers are honest and work hard. The best rule, if in any doubt about whether to take a particular cab, is to flag down another. That was what a Thai once told me to do in such cases. Applies in all countries, not just Thailand.

Motor cycle taxis are faster and cheaper. But their weaving in and out of traffic may or may not appeal to you.

Outside Bangkok, the usual form of transport is the *sawngtaew* (literally, two benches). They are converted pick-up trucks that carry around ten people (more, if you want to stand on the rear platform – but do hang on tightly.) They normally charge passengers the same fare irrespective of distance and plan the journey depending on where passengers want to go. Because they don't run on fixed routes, they may decline a fare if they are not going your way. You won't normally have to wait long for another *sawngtaew*.

In small villages, you can see motor cycle sidecars that can take two or three passengers for short distances. Pedal rickshaws are slow and not as popular today as they were; but they are a pleasant way of taking in the sights if you are on the tourist trail. Lampang has horse drawn carriages used by tourists and locals.

For longer distances, travelling by air, coach, or train are options. Trains are slow and often run on single tracks, so delays of several hours are not uncommon. Buses are faster but do not have good safety records.

23 June

I know Tong works hard at her job in the government office where she works. With twenty years' experience, she has a reputation as a dedicated employee, working late to finish the tasks she has set herself for the day. Her annual reviews have always been exemplary up until now.

The job appraisal system is complicated. The scoring method gives credit for exceptional skills, progress on training courses, adaptability, job knowledge, and teamwork. Her results are on a par with previous years.

Why does her new boss now give her an average of 50% when the individual scores range from 75 to 95 as in previous years? Is some envy creeping in because in the past she has had some very good salary increases? Tong's qualifications put her very close to the salary her boss gets.

Her husband, Oh, runs his own successful construction company and works long hours to ensure it succeeds. With Tong working just as hard, their joint incomes give them a good lifestyle. They went to Edinburgh last year and holidayed in Japan the year before. They work hard and play hard.
Government employees in Thailand need a confirmation letter to travel abroad. It's not been a problem before, but this year the application for traveling to France seemed to hit lots of administrative snags. She got approval eventually but it left a nasty

taste in her mouth that her boss was being so awkward. *Khun* Sompanya, now very unpopular, has been in post less than one year and has never been abroad herself.

Do Thais have a jealous streak?

I suggested that Tong ask for a meeting with her boss about the delays to her vacation approval and more importantly her job evaluation.

"That would seem like a challenge to my boss's position, Matt. Everyone has a place in the office hierarchy. I will get some colleagues to drop a few well-chosen comments about my work and how it compares with the performance of others; but I can do no more than that. Thais like to use an intermediary to resolve a problem rather than going direct. I know that sounds strange to Westerners, Matt."

20 May

What I notice most about the Thais is that they smile a lot. It's the impression everyone gets when they first come here.

They don't talk loudly and detest aggressive language and behaviour. Quarrels and disagreements are anathema to the Thais. They have a laid-back hassle free lifestyle (*mai pen rai*) and come across as having a very caring and helpful attitude.

Family and community is important to them and they will seize any opportunity to be with other people.

The other side of Thailand, which is a bit of an enigma, is the corruption and violence that is endemic in the culture. Corruption is seen as normal, as part of one's salary and part of everyday commercial life. It is changing but changing slowly. Violence can stem from a distrust of impartial law enforcement. Disputes are usually handled locally.

At times, Thailand is a perfect paradise on earth, at others; it can be a dangerous den of deception, dishonesty, and deviousness.

Thais dislike criticism of themselves and their country and are patriotic to the point of xenophobia. I always try to avoid saying or doing anything that makes them feel they are losing face. It is not easy to be direct, firm, fair, and tactful at the same time. Praise should be laid on with a shovel when it is necessary, as indeed the Thais do. That helps.